Every Day with Jesus

SEP/OCT 2019

Teach Us to Pray

'Our Father in heaven, hallowed be your name'
Matthew 6:9

Selwyn Hughes
Revised and updated by Mick Brooks

© CWR 2019. Dated text previously published as *The Lord's Prayer* (Jul/August 1983) by CWR. This edition revised and updated for 2019 by Mick Brooks.

CWR, Waverley Abbey House, Waverley Lane, Farnham, Surrey GU9 8EP, UK **Tel: 01252 784700**
Email: mail@cwr.org.uk Registered Charity No. 294387. Registered Limited Company No. 1990308.

Where possible, every effort has been made to ensure that these devotional notes contain the correct permissions and references. Please contact the Publisher directly for any further permissions information.

Cover image: Stocksy/Victor Torres
Quiet Time image: Adobestock/Toeytoey
Printed in England by Linney

CWR

Every Day with Jesus is available in large print from CWR. It is also available on **audio and DAISY** in the UK and Eire for the sole use of those with a visual impairment worse than N12, or who are registered blind. For details please contact **Torch Trust for the Blind**, Tel: 01858 438260. Torch House, Torch Way, Northampton Road, Market Harborough LE16 9HL.

A word of introduction...

Prayer. Does it make your heart sink or soar? So much has been written, spoken, taught and instructed on what is considered a vital topic. There are literally thousands of quotes extoling the importance and necessity of prayer, such as: 'Prayer should be the key of the day and the lock of the night' – George Herbert. 'If you only pray when you're in trouble, you're in trouble' – Anonymous. 'No man is greater than his prayer life' – Leonard Ravenhill. 'Prayer is man's greatest power' – W. Clement Stone. 'To get nations back on their feet, we must first get down on our knees' – Billy Graham. 'To pray well is the better half of study' – Martin Luther.

For some, these quotes will energise and encourage; others will feel burdened and troubled. Most days we all want to pray more, and at the same time, we sometimes feel we don't pray enough or for the right things. I personally would love to have been there when the disciples asked Jesus, 'Lord, teach us to pray', to hear His response and answers to their further questions. Fortunately, their conversation was recorded for us by those present and His answers will be the focus of our meditations this issue. My prayer for us all is that prayer will not be a task to be completed but we will it experience it like Moses did when God spoke with him like a friend (Exod. 33:11).

God bless,

Mick

Mick Brooks, Consulting Editor

A pattern for prayer

FOR READING & MEDITATION – MATTHEW 6:1–13

'This, then, is how you should pray: "Our Father in heaven, hallowed be your name"' (v9)

Today we begin an exciting exploration of one of the most well known and most often recited passages in the whole of the New Testament: the Lord's Prayer. These words of Jesus, so seemingly simple, encompass the great mystery of prayer and translate it into a practical pattern.

The Lord's Prayer (or, more correctly, the Disciples' Prayer) is, among other things, a miracle of condensation. In the short compass of 66 words, Jesus presents a model of praying that touches on every major aspect of prayer. One writer says of it: 'The Lord's Prayer sets the standard for all praying. Everything everyone ever needed to understand about prayer is latent in the choice disclosure of these words.' That might sound like an astonishing claim, but it is true. No set of theological volumes, no sermon, no series of writings has ever captured the fullness of all that prayer is and does as this simple and yet profound model.

The more we understand this model, and the more we pray in line with it, the more relational and revelatory our prayer life will become. Our relationship with God, as we have said many times before, begins with prayer. The importance of this communication is underlined in Luke's account of the Lord's Prayer, where the disciples, on seeing Jesus pray on one occasion, asked Him, 'Lord, teach us to pray' (Luke 11:1). The Lord's Prayer helps us remember our priorities, keeps us focused on God and enables us to pray according to His will. If this is how Jesus answered His disciples' question, then we too would do well to understand this pattern in order that our prayers might become more and more like His.

FURTHER STUDY

1 Tim. 2:1–8;
1 Chron. 16:11;
Luke 18:1;
1 Thess. 5:17

1. What was Christ's injunction?

2. What is Paul's exhortation?

Lord God, as I begin this quest for a deeper and more effective prayer life, my heart cries out: 'Lord, teach me to pray.' For I know that when I learn to pray, I learn to live – vitally and victoriously. Amen.

More than a recitation

FOR READING & MEDITATION – MATTHEW 6:7–18

'And when you pray, do not keep on babbling... for they think they will be heard because of their many words.' (v7)

If we are to grow in our relationship with God and pray in accordance with God's will then, as we considered yesterday, we need to learn to bring our prayers in line with the principles laid down in the marvellous model given to us by Jesus, which we affectionately call the Lord's Prayer.

Some think that prayer consists solely in reciting the words of the Lord's Prayer but, as the great preacher C.H. Spurgeon once said, 'To recite the Lord's Prayer and believe that you have then prayed is the height of foolishness.' This does not mean, of course, that there is no spiritual value in reciting it, providing we realise that it is not just a prayer to be recited. Personally, I would not want to deprive people of the pleasure of reciting together the Lord's Prayer and perhaps in some cases re-igniting the memory of it. Nevertheless, I do want to encourage the view that it is a departure point rather than an arrival platform.

FURTHER STUDY

Gal. 4:1–11;
Isa. 29:13;
Matt. 6:5

1. What is Paul saying about ritualism?

2. When does prayer become hypocritical?

If Jesus advised His disciples to avoid 'babbling like pagans' when they prayed, would He then immediately follow it by giving us a prayer to simply recite, and nothing more? As I have said, one can derive great comfort and pleasure from repeating the words that Jesus gave us, but if we are to gain the greatest value from the Lord's Prayer, then we are to view it as a skeleton on which we have to put flesh. If we view these words not merely as something to recite together but as an outline we work our way through when praying, no matter what we are praying about, then we will experience a growing confidence that we are praying the way Jesus taught. You see, it's one thing to recite a prayer: it's another thing to know how to pray.

Heavenly Father, I see there can be great value in reciting a prayer, but I want to be able to do more than repeat a prayer – I want to pray. Help me, for without You I can do nothing. Amen.

FOR READING & MEDITATION – LUKE 11:1–13

'This, then, is how you should pray "Our Father in heaven, hallowed be your name"' (Matt. 6:9)

We've been considering the significance and importance of the Lord's Prayer. Today we look at the first word with which the prayer begins: 'Our'. That first word determines the very nature of the Christian faith. Suppose it had been 'My'? That would have changed the whole nature of the Christian faith. Instead of our faith being 'our'-centred it would have been 'my'-centred – and that would have started us off wrong.

In the field of prayer, as in many other fields, to start wrong is to finish wrong. The word 'our' involves a shifting of emphasis from me to the Father, and to my brothers and sisters in the kingdom. It implies that we no longer put ourselves first but, rather, we remind ourselves of our relationship to God as our Father and that we are part of the kingdom of heaven. The first Beatitude describes the foundational characteristic of those who belong to that kingdom as 'poor in spirit' (Matt. 5:3). So, implied in the first words of the Lord's Prayer is the repositioning that a disciple of Jesus has come to: an attitude of self-surrender – surrender to the Father, and to His interests, and the interests of others in His kingdom. When we do this, everything begins to open to us. The rest of the Lord's Prayer has no meaning and dies if the 'Our' is not alive.

And what does this mean? It means that the 'Our' must reach far beyond our own fellowship, local church or denomination to include the whole family of God – everywhere. It is hard to grasp and enter into God's greater plan for the whole unless we come to it prepared to sacrifice self-interest and embrace the 'our'.

FURTHER STUDY

Luke 18:9–14; Mark 10:35–44; Matt. 23:12

1. How did Jesus answer James and John?

2. What was wrong with the Pharisee's prayer?

Father, cleanse my heart from any limitations I might have in relation to the word 'Our'. Help me to make it a true 'Our' with everybody including those who are different to me. In Jesus' name. Amen.

A family within a family

FOR READING & MEDITATION – JOHN 1:1–13

*'to all who received him, to those who believed in his name, he gave
the right to become children of God' (v12)*

Today we examine the second word which appears in Jesus' model of prayer – 'Father'. In Christian circles, the term 'Father' is probably the most common term we use when addressing God, and rightly so, for this is the pattern Jesus set when teaching His disciples the art of effective praying. Our focus and prayer begin with the recognition that God is our Father.

This raises the much-debated question: is God a Father to all people everywhere, or only to those who have given and committed their lives to God? Some liberal theologians and philosophers have taught that God is everyone's Father. The logical outcome of this teaching is that all of humankind must be His children and, therefore, we are all brothers and sisters of one another. In my view, this approach, sometimes referred to as the universal brotherhood of man, makes conversion unnecessary and puts to one side the redemptive sufferings of Christ on the cross.

FURTHER STUDY

Rom. 8:1–17;
Psa. 68:5;
Isa. 64:8

1. How have we 'received the Spirit of sonship'?

2. What is our cry?

The Bible identifies that God is a Father in two senses. First, He is the Father of the human family by virtue of creation. Malachi 2:10 says: 'Have we not all one Father? Did not one God create us?' In Acts 17:29 Paul said, 'We are God's offspring'. In the sense of creation, yes, God is our Father. However, in the sense of a familial relationship, He is not. Jesus said in John 8:44 to the Jewish leaders: 'You belong to your father, the devil.' Frequently, the Fatherhood of God is seen in the Bible in two senses. He is the Father of all men and women because He is their creator, but He has another family – a family within a family – consisting of those who have committed themselves to Jesus Christ, the Son.

Lord God, I am so grateful that I know You as my Father – not only in the creative sense, but also in the familial sense. May the wonder of this closer relationship grow within me hour by hour and day by day. For Jesus' sake. Amen.

CWR Ministry Events

PLEASE PRAY FOR THE TEAM

DATE	EVENT	PLACE	PRESENTER(S)
3–5 Sep	Waverley Access Course	Waverley Abbey House	WAC team
5 Sep	Meeting Pastoral Care Challenges	WAH	Andy Peck
6–8 Sep	Bible Discovery Weekend	WAH	Philip Greenslade
20–22	Inspiring Women Autumn Weekend: Belonging	WAH	Ems Hancock and Rosie Morgan
25 Sep	Discovering Your Spiritual Gifts	WAH	Andy Peck
3 Oct	Knowing Jesus	WAH	Andy Peck
9 Oct	Inspiring Women Autumn Day	WAH	Jen Baker
14–18 Oct	Woman to Woman	WAH	Inspiring Women team
16 Oct	Understanding the Bible and the Supernatural	WAH	Andy Peck
23 Oct	The Spirit-Filled Life	WAH	Andy Peck
28 Oct – 1 Nov	Introduction to Christian Care and Counselling	WAH	Louise Dyer and team

Please pray for our students and tutors on our ongoing BA Counselling programme at Waverley Abbey College (which takes place at Waverley Abbey House), as well as our Certificate in Christian Counselling and MA Counselling qualifications.

We would also appreciate prayer for our ongoing ministry in Singapore and Cambodia, as well as the many regional events that will be happening around the UK this year.

For further information and a full list of CWR's courses, seminars and events, call **(+44) 01252 784719** or visit **cwr.org.uk/courses**

You can also download our free Prayer Track, which includes daily prayers, from **cwr.org.uk/prayertrack**

God is a Father

FOR READING & MEDITATION – 1 JOHN 2:1–15

'I write to you... because you have known the Father.' (v13)

W e said yesterday that God is a Father in two senses, the creative sense and the familial sense. This leads me to ask for whom was the Lord's Prayer designed – for everyone, or only God's redeemed children? There is no doubt in my mind that it was intended for Jesus' true disciples, those whose lives are committed to Him and to His cause. Clearly many people outside the Christian Church find the words greatly comforting, but much of the appeal is sentimental rather than spiritual.

To understand the Lord's Prayer, and apply its principles in the way Jesus intended, one needs to have experienced a genuine conversion. Then, and only then, does its true meaning become apparent. Jesus shows us in the first sentence of His prayer pattern that true discipleship begins with a concept of God as Father. Someone has pointed out that the term 'Father' answers all the philosophical questions about the nature of God. A father is a person, therefore God is not an invisible force behind the machinery of the universe. A father is able to hear, therefore God is not an impersonal being, aloof from all our troubles and trials. And, above all, a father is predisposed, by reason of his familial relationship, to give careful attention to what his child says.

FURTHER STUDY

John 5:17–47;
1:12;
2 Cor. 6:17–18;
Gal. 4:5–6

1. How did Jesus speak of His Father?

2. What is God's promise to those who believe?

When we pray, then, to the Father, we must hold in our minds the picture of our eternal creator as someone who has a father's heart, a father's love and a father's disposition. This, then, is the second note we strike when praying – God is a Father, and we can come to Him with all the trust, confidence, openness and frankness of a child.

Lord God, I am so grateful that in the word 'Father' I discover the greatest truth about You. My heart rests itself on that glorious and wonderful truth. Thank You, Father. Amen.

FOR READING & MEDITATION – HEBREWS 11:1–6

'anyone who comes to him must believe that he exists and that he rewards those who earnestly seek him.' (v6)

We continue meditating on the second word of the Lord's Prayer – 'Father'. It is not enough that we address God as 'Father', simply saying the word with our lips. If we misunderstand the nature of God's Fatherhood, it will be very difficult to pray the way Jesus laid down for us. I have said before that no one can rise higher in their prayer life than their concept of God. If you do not hold in your heart a picture of God as He really is, then your prayers will be short-circuited and, like electricity when it has nowhere else to go, will run into the earth.

What goes on in your thoughts and feelings when the word 'father' is mentioned? Some will have positive thoughts and feelings like warmth, love, affection; while others will experience negative feelings such as remoteness, sternness, or even unconcern. For many people, the word 'father' has to be redeemed or rewritten, because it conjures up memories of unhappy or difficult or distant relationships. I believe that this is why Jesus, after laying down the structure of prayer in Luke 11, then went on to teach us, through the parable of the friend who came at midnight, just what God is really like. He is not only a Father, said Jesus, but also a friend.

Jesus, knowing that for some the word 'father' would have negative connotations, attempted to fill it with a deeper content, by revealing that God was a Father and a friend. We need to ensure our concept of the word 'father' is true and healthy, for if it isn't, then to approach Him with the confidence of a trusting child will remain a constant struggle.

FURTHER STUDY

John 11:5–36; 15:13–15; 14:18; Prov. 18:24

1. How did Jesus show true friendship?

2. To what length was this demonstrated?

Dear God, I see that my prayer life rises or falls in relation to my understanding of Your Fatherhood. Give me a vision of Your loving care and concern for me that will enable me to come to You in childlike trust and confidence. Amen.

Jesus reveals the Father

FOR READING & MEDITATION – JOHN 14:1–14

'Anyone who has seen me has seen the Father.' (v9)

We touched yesterday on what I believe is one of the most important truths we can ever discover in relation to prayer, namely, that we will never rise higher in our prayer lives than our understanding and concept of God. Time and time again, I have watched people struggle over this issue. Their prayers remain hesitant because, deep down in their hearts, they doubt God's willingness to respond to them.

This is why, if we are to learn to pray the Jesus way, it's important to seek to develop a clear understanding of the Fatherhood of God. But how can we gain a picture of God's Fatherhood that is true to reality? One way we do it is by focusing upon Jesus. God is a relational Father. The Jews referred to God using lofty and exalted titles. Jesus must have stunned them all when He used the Aramaic word 'Abba' used by children to call their fathers 'daddy'. Jesus went on to say in John 14:9: 'Anyone who has seen me has seen the Father.'

FURTHER STUDY

John 17;
10:25–42; 5:17;
Luke 2:49

1. How did Jesus show He was of the Father?

2. What did Jesus pray?

'The philosophies of India', said one writer, 'are the high watermark of man's search for God. Here the mind of man strained itself to search for God and speculate about Him. But in all their searching, they never discovered that He was a loving and tender Father. And why? Because they had no Jesus. They had Rama, Krishna, Shankara, Buddha, and many others, but no Jesus.' That lack was the vital lack. For Jesus is the expression of the Father in human form. If you want to know what God is like as a Father, then gaze at Jesus. He clears the fog and misconceptions from around God and shows us that the heart that beats at the back of the universe is like His heart – a heart overflowing with unconditional love.

Lord Jesus, I am so thankful that I no longer need wonder what the Father is like; He is like You. You have revealed Him as He truly is. This gives a clear focus to my praying. I am deeply grateful. Amen.

Getting the right focus

FOR READING & MEDITATION – ISAIAH 40:25–31

'Lift your eyes and look... Who created all these?' (v26)

Having spent this past week examining the first two words of the Lord's Prayer, we turn now to focus on the next two words: 'in heaven'. It might seem astonishing that we can spend a whole week meditating on just a few words of this matchless prayer, but one of the wonders of Scripture is its ability to introduce us to vast themes with a minimum of words. In the Lord's Prayer, a library is compressed into a phrase; a volume squeezed into a single syllable. These inspired words and phrases have become the source of numerous writings and expositions, yet none of them, this one included, can fully plumb the depths of all that Jesus was expounding.

We now ask ourselves: what was Jesus wanting us to grasp when He taught His disciples to pray, 'Our Father in heaven…'? He wanted to teach them (so I believe) the way to achieve a true perspective in prayer. Before we can pray effectively, we are first to be convinced who God is (our Father) and where God is (in heaven). In other words, again the initial focus of our praying is not on ourselves but on God.

Doesn't this reveal at once a fatal weakness in our praying? We come into God's presence and instead of focusing our gaze upon Him, we focus it on our issues and our struggles and questions; we are told that our thoughts are like magnifying glasses and whatever we turn our thoughts to we magnify. This only serves to increase the awareness of our lack. Perhaps this is why, when praying, we can end up more confused or more frustrated than when we began? This is perhaps one of the greatest lessons we can learn about prayer – our initial focus should always be upon God.

FURTHER STUDY

Isa. 40:12–24;
Psa. 123:1;
John 11:41; 17:1;
Acts 7:55

1. How does Isaiah enlarge our vision of God?

2. What did Jesus do when He prayed?

Lord God, I begin to see now where I have lost focus in this vital matter of prayer. I have begun with myself, instead of beginning with You. Help me to get the right initial position in my praying. In Jesus' name. Amen.

'Imagineering'

FOR READING & MEDITATION – ISAIAH 26:1–13

'Thou wilt keep him in perfect peace, whose mind [imagination] is stayed on thee' (v3, KJV)

We saw yesterday that one of the most important lessons we can learn about prayer is that of getting our initial focus right. We focus upon God before we begin to focus on ourselves. How many times, when making an approach to God in prayer, have we gone immediately into a series of petitions that have to do with our problems, our difficulties, our circumstances? And so, by focusing our attention on what is troubling us, we end up wondering whether or not God is big enough, or strong enough, to help us.

FURTHER STUDY

1 Cor. 2:1–16;
Gen. 6:5;
Rom. 1:21;
2 Cor. 10:5

1. How can we 'demolish arguments'?

2. What has God given to us?

In the first four words of the Lord's Prayer, Jesus shows us a better way. He tells us to take a slow, calm, reassuring gaze at God – at His tenderness, His eagerness to give, His unwearying patience and untiring love. The result of this, of course, is that we develop a calmness and tranquillity in our spirit, which means we will find it no longer necessary to plunge into a panicky flood of words.

In some parts of the world, one can enrol in courses called 'Imagineering' – courses that are designed to stimulate creative imagination. Many of our problems begin in the imagination – hence the instruction in the words of our text for today. 'One can never become proficient in prayer', said one writer, 'until the imagination has been redeemed.' What did he mean? He meant that when the imagination is redeemed from self-concentration, sex-concentration, sin-concentration, and makes God its prime focus, then it becomes creative-conscious, since its attention is concentrated on the creator and the re-creator. And when the imagination is redeemed, all the doors of the personality fly open.

Lord God, help me become calm and tranquil, and help my imagination be more God-centred than self-centred. Help me to be a God-focused person, not only at prayer times, but at all times. Amen.

God's 'postal address'

FOR READING & MEDITATION – PSALM 20:1–9

'he answers him from his holy heaven' (v6)

We continue meditating on why Jesus, in the opening words of the Lord's Prayer, taught us to focus first on God before presenting to Him our petitions.

Today we ask ourselves: why did Jesus bid us pray, 'Our Father in heaven'? What is so important about the fact that God lives in heaven? Someone has suggested that heaven is God's 'postal address' and, therefore, the place to which all prayers and petitions are to be directed. I believe, however, that Jesus, in using the words 'in heaven', sought to focus our minds, not so much on God's location, but rather His elevation. We are so used to living, as we say, 'with an earthly view', surrounded by limitations and restrictions, that we are apt to forget that God exists in heaven, a place where there are no shortages and no restraints. Here, on earth, we stagger from one crisis to another, face endless problems, economic recessions, strikes, political unrest, and so on, but in heaven, such situations are non-existent. There are no shortages in the factories of His grace, no disputes on His assembly lines and no faults in His communication system. Because of Christ's sacrifice on Calvary we have access, at any time of day or night, into God's presence. There is no waiting, no 'leave a message and we'll get back to you', you'll be put straight through to the King of kings!

When Jesus asks us to focus on God who is in heaven, He is reminding us to elevate our spiritual vision until it breaks free of earth's gravitational pull, and to remind ourselves constantly of the truth that, in our Father's presence, our greatest problems turn into possibilities.

FURTHER STUDY

Rev. 21;
Isa. 66:1–2;
Matt. 5:34;
Rev. 4:2

1. What is the focal point of heaven?

2. How does this elevate our vision?

Father, this phrase 'in heaven' is like a rocket that launches me beyond earth's limitations into a place where everything is peace and light. Help me never lose sight of this fact – today and every day. Amen.

Settling down in God

FOR READING & MEDITATION – ISAIAH 6:1–8

'I saw the Lord seated on a throne, high and exalted' (v1)

We continue meditating on the words 'in heaven' used by Jesus in His model prayer. We said yesterday that these words are intended to help us focus, not only on God's location, but also on His elevation. The Saviour (so I believe) encourages us, when we come to God in prayer, to get our perspective right, and to look above 'the ragged edges of time' to the heights of eternity where God has His royal throne.

The old Welsh preachers and theologians such as Christmas Evans, Daniel Rowlands, and others, used to call this aspect of prayer 'settling down in God'. They taught that when we gain a right perspective of God and heavenly things then, and only then, can we have a right perspective of man and earthly things. It is noteworthy that it was after King Uzziah died that Isaiah saw his vision in the temple of the Lord 'high and exalted' and that he was able to put into focus the events that were happening around him. Our life here on earth will never be abundant until we realise that we have access to resources which are outside of terrestrial thinking and things.

FURTHER STUDY

Matt. 19:13–26;
Eph. 3:20;
2 Cor. 9:8;
Phil. 4:19

1. What was the declaration of Jesus?

2. How did Paul describe 'El-Shaddai'?

I have said, on a previous occasion, that a good working translation of the term El-Shaddai (Gen. 17:1) is 'God – the Enough'. Actually, of course, He is more than enough, but how comforting it is to know that He is at least that. So, when coming to God in prayer, learn to settle yourself down in God. Remind yourself that His resources so infinitely exceed your requirements; His sufficiency so immeasurably surpasses every call you may make upon it. Get the divine perspective right and earthly things will fall into their right and proper focus.

My Father, gently and quietly I breathe the strength of Your presence into every portion of my being. I realise that when I see You 'high and exalted', then all of life is reduced to its proper proportions. I am so thankful. Amen.

'Too close to the ground'

FOR READING & MEDITATION – PSALM 92:1–15

'But you, O LORD, are exalted for ever.' (v8)

Quietly, as we study these two words from the Lord's Prayer, we are coming to the conclusion that before we can see clearly the events of time in their proper perspective, we need to learn to focus our gaze upon God. Possibly the reason why our personal questions and struggles seem so onerous is due mainly to the fact that we have not brought God into proper focus. When we see Him as He really is – 'high and exalted' – then all our troubles and questions are reduced to their proper proportions.

A minister looked through his study window one day into the garden next door. He saw a little boy there, holding in his hand two pieces of wood, each about 18 inches long. He heard him ask his mother if he could make a weathervane. After getting her permission, he proceeded to nail one piece of wood upright on the low garden wall, then nailed the other piece loosely on top. Soon the loosely nailed piece of wood turned and twisted, first this way and then that, and the little boy danced with delight. He thought he had a weathervane that registered the winds, but all it did was register the draughts. 'It turned half a circle,' said the minister, 'when the back door banged.'

FURTHER STUDY

Psa. 8:1–9;
1 Cor. 13:12;
2 Cor. 3:18

1. How did the psalmist focus his gaze on God?

2. How did Paul describe it?

From where the minister sat in his study, he could see a real weathervane on the church steeple. It was as steady as a rock in the constant winds that blew in from the sea. There are many Christians, however, who are like the little boy's weathervane – at the mercy of every gust of circumstance, their thoughts of God fluctuating with their personal experiences. They take their direction from a weathervane that is too close to the ground.

God my Father, forgive me that I'm taken up more with the immediate than the ultimate. I have been glancing at You and gazing at my circumstances. From today it will be different – I will glance at my circumstances and gaze at You. Amen.

The universe proclaims it

FOR READING & MEDITATION – PSALM 19:1–14

'The heavens declare the glory of God' (v1)

We are endeavouring this week, in line with Jesus' directive in the Lord's Prayer, to focus our gaze on the majesty, the omnipotence and the greatness of God. The greater God becomes in our gaze, the more realistically we will be able to evaluate the events that go on around us here on earth.

In the passage we have read today the psalmist tells us that one way we can focus on the greatness of God is to consider His handiwork in creation. All around us in this wonderful world we see evidences of His eternal power and divine nature by the things He has made. Consider, for example, the vastness of the universe. Scientists tell us that in relation to the myriads of other celestial bodies in outer space, the planet we inhabit is like a tiny speck of dust in one of the huge London railway stations in comparison to all the other specks of dust around it, or like a single grain of sand among all the other grains of sand on all the seashores of the world. They tell us also that if the earth were to fall out of its orbit and spin away into space, it would create no more disturbance than a single drop in the Pacific Ocean!

FURTHER STUDY

Matt. 6:19–34;
Luke 12:24;
Psa. 45:1–17

1, How did Jesus focus our attention on God's goodness?

2. Of whom does the psalmist give us a picture?

Such word pictures, inadequate as they are, nevertheless help us form some idea of the greatness and transcendence of our God. Who can meditate on the vastness of the universe without experiencing an expansion in their conception of the majesty of God? I have often pondered on why God constructed the universe on such a grand scale, and my conclusion is this – He did it to show us that He is gloriously sufficient, unchangingly adequate and abidingly faithful.

Father God, thank You that I can depend on You and that Your resources never run dry. Help me to live in the light of the truth, that You are God the Enough. I am so thankful. Amen.

National **Prayer** Weekend

27–29 September 2019

If reading through this issue on the Lord's Prayer is getting you exciting about praying, why not join in with this year's National Prayer Weekend? There are so many Christians across the UK who are expectant for what God is going to do, and the good news is it's not too late to sign up if you would like to join us!

Already taking part?

Don't forget to visit the NPW website and make the most of the prayer resources on offer – whether to share with those you pray for or to help engage people with your event. There are also books for children and young people, to guide them as they explore prayer for themselves.

Not yet signed up?

Head to the website and put your pin on the map! You can join in as an individual, with a prayer partner, group, or even your whole church – just register your postcode so we know you're praying.

Want to support NPW in other ways?

Why not pray for the people praying? To get involved on social media and join the community, use and follow the hashtag #NPW2019 and find out more by following @NPWtogether on Twitter.

To find out more, visit
national-prayer-weekend.com

A time exposure to God

FOR READING & MEDITATION – PSALM 62:1–12

'One thing God has spoken, two things have I heard: that you, O God, are strong, and that you, O Lord, are loving.' (vv11–12)

Over the past week we have been considering the effect of presenting our requests to God before pausing to reflect on His unchanging adequacy and sufficiency. We said that one reason why Jesus directed us to use the words 'in heaven' was to encourage us to focus our gaze on a God who is unaffected by the restrictions and limitations of earth, and who dwells in a place where the resources never run dry.

Those who plunge into the areas of petition and intercession, before reflecting on the abundant resources that lie in God, will find their praying limited and more in tune with themselves than God. As one poet says:

FURTHER STUDY

Eph. 1;
Psa. 5:3;
65:5–7;
1 Chron. 29:12

1. What was Paul's prayer for the Ephesians?

2. Ask God to enlarge your vision in this way.

*'What a frail soul he gave me, and a heart
Lame and unlikely for the large events.'*

However, I wonder if, more often than not, we have given ourselves 'a heart lame and unlikely for the large events' because we rush into God's presence to present our petitions before taking stock of our spiritual resources.

God offers us infinite resources for the asking and the taking – Himself. The first moments of prayer are often best spent in an attitude of contemplation, reflection and meditation. As we gaze upon God and His infinite resources, we take, as someone put it, 'a time exposure to God'. His adequacy and sufficiency are printed indelibly upon us. No matter, then, what difficulties and problems face us – He is more than a match for them. The vision of His greatness puts the whole of life in its proper perspective: 'We kneel, how weak – we rise, how full of power.'

Father, I am so thankful that my resources are so near at hand. I reflect on Your greatness and wonder in the depths of my heart, and my praying takes on new strength and power. I am so grateful. Amen.

Honouring God's name

FOR READING & MEDITATION – JOHN 14:12–21

'I will do whatever you ask in my name, so that the Son may bring glory to the Father.' (v13)

We come now to the next clause in Jesus' pattern of prayer: 'hallowed be your name'. We ask ourselves: what does it mean to hallow the name of our loving heavenly Father? Remembering that Jesus is nearly always more concerned that we seek God's 'face' before we seek His 'hand', to hallow God's name once again causes us to not rush into our requests, but to pause and focus on our Father in heaven. To hallow something is to reverence it or treat it as sacred. It is derived from a very important word in the Bible (Greek: *hagiazo*) which means to venerate, set apart, to make holy. Does this mean that our veneration of God makes Him holy? No, for nothing we do can add to His qualities or attributes, and nothing we do can subtract from them. God is the only being in the universe who needs nothing, or no one, to complete Him. To venerate God simply means to recognise who He really is. This way prayer becomes much more than a way by which we can talk to God about our problems and difficulties: it is a vehicle by which God can increasingly reveal to us who He is and who we are.

FURTHER STUDY

John 1:1–14;
13:31; 17:4;
1 Pet. 4:11

1. What was John's testimony of Christ?

2. What was Jesus' testimony of Himself?

This might surprise some who think of prayer merely as a means by which they can obtain things from God. However, prayer, first and foremost, is a relationship in which God is able to be known and through which He can reveal the awesome extent of His deep love and concern for us, and that we in turn will know ourselves better. And as we get to know our Father, our requests will become more in line with His will and bring glory to His name. Isn't it amazing that the first petition in the Lord's Prayer is not for our own behalf but for His?

Lord God, help me to build my prayer life according to the pattern that Jesus gave me, and begin by deepening the conviction that my first petition should not be for myself but for You and Your eternal glory. Amen.

What's in a name?

FOR READING & MEDITATION – EXODUS 34:1–10

'Then the LORD... proclaimed his name... the compassionate and gracious God, slow to anger, abounding in love' (vv5–7)

We ended yesterday by saying that the first petition in the Lord's Prayer is not for our behalf but for God's – 'hallowed be your name'. Arthur W. Pink says in his book *An Exposition of the Sermon on the Mount*: 'How clearly, then, is the fundamental duty of prayer set forth: self, and all its needs, must be given a secondary place, and the Lord freely accorded the pre-eminence in our thoughts, desires and supplications. This petition [hallowed be your name] must take the precedence, for the glory of God's great name is the ultimate end of all things.'

FURTHER STUDY

Psa. 111:1–10;
138:2;
Lev. 22:2;
Isa. 29:23

1. How does the psalmist link God's name and acts?

2. What does 'reverence' mean?

Today we ask ourselves: what does it mean to hallow God's name? Are we required to pronounce God's name in the quietest and most reverent of tones? Does it mean that we develop a mystical attitude towards the name of God? I do not believe so. In biblical times, names were not just designations, but definitions. They had varied and special meanings. A name represented a person's character, such as is demonstrated in 1 Samuel 18:30: 'David... behaved himself more wisely than all Saul's servants, so that his name was very dear and highly esteemed' (Amplified). The people did not esteem the letters of David's name. The statement means that David himself was esteemed.

In the text for today we are given not just the name of God, but some of the characteristics that go under that name. He is compassionate, gracious, slow to anger, abounding in love and faithfulness, and so on. In other words, when we pray 'hallowed be your name', that name represents the composite of all God's attributes. When we honour God's name, we honour Him and we in turn will be honoured (see 1 Sam. 2:30).

Father, I begin to see that my purpose in prayer has been to get the things I thought I needed. Now I realise my greatest need is to give You the first place You deserve. Write this vital truth on my heart, I pray. Amen.

'Jehovah' – no such word

FOR READING & MEDITATION – EXODUS 3:1–15
'God said to Moses, "I AM WHO I AM."' (v14)

We continue meditating on what it means to honour or revere the name of God. We saw yesterday that it is not just esteeming the letters in His name, nor speaking His name in hushed or quiet tones. The ancient Israelites attached such a sacredness to the name of God that they would not say it aloud. They thought that hallowing God's name meant hallowing the name itself. While they paid honour to the actual letters of God's name they, on occasions, thought nothing about disobeying His word and denying His truth.

Hebrew scholars point out that there is no such word as Jehovah in the Hebrew language, although it appears in English translations of the Old Testament. The name of God in Exodus 3:14, where the Almighty gave His name to Moses, I AM WHO I AM, is Yahweh: the English equivalent of which is Jehovah. The Israelites would not say the word Yahweh, and eventually the vowels were taken out and mixed with the consonants of another Hebrew word to form the word Adonai. This was done as a device to avoid having to say the real word 'Yahweh'. While the motive behind this convoluted reasoning was out of reverence for God's name, what is more important is a heart that is right with God (see Matt. 15:7–8).

When Jesus taught us to pray 'hallowed be your name', He meant that God's name stands for who He is – His self-existence, His mercy, His compassion, His love, His grace, His power, and so on. When, as God's children, we come to Him to honour His name, we do more than enter into a religious routine – we contemplate all that His name stands for, and reverence Him for who He is.

FURTHER STUDY

Gen. 17:1; 22:14;
Exod. 15:26;
17:15;
Judg. 6:24;
Psa. 23:1;
Jer. 23:6;
Ezek. 48:35

1. What are some names of God?

2. What do they mean?

Father, I see that true prayer is not just a technique, it is a relationship. Help me to develop that relationship, and to apply all You are teaching me in my prayer life day by day. Amen.

In line with God's character

FOR READING & MEDITATION – MATTHEW 26:36–46

'Yet not as I will, but as you will.' (v39)

We are seeing from our examination of Jesus' words in the Lord's Prayer – 'hallowed be your name' – that our first consideration, when approaching God, is the reverence and recognition of His name. And why His name? Because His name stands for all He is. When we reverence His name, we take into consideration all the aspects of His nature and character.

Let's pause together and briefly remind ourselves of just a few of His characteristics that we discover in the Scriptures. He is infinite – we cannot define Him by proportions or magnitude. He has no beginning, no end, and no limits. He spoke all things into being, and all things – from the smallest to the most magnificent – are sustained by Him. He is the embodiment of perfect goodness. He is kind, full of favour towards all of creation. He is love: God's love is so great that He gave His only Son to bring us back into relationship with Him and God's love embraces each of us personally and intimately. God is transcendent – existing beyond and above the created universe. More than anything we can possibly imagine God is righteous and holy, fair and equitable in all things. We can trust Him to always do what is right. He is merciful: God's merciful compassion is never-ending and does not run dry. God is faithful: He honours His covenants and fulfils His promises (Eph. 1:5–8).

When we stop and consider all He is, it helps us put God's character first and our requests for our needs second – putting both in the right place. True prayer begins with God, puts self in a secondary place, and seeks to honour and glorify God's name. It is characterised by a desire for God's will more than our own will.

FURTHER STUDY

Rom. 12;
Exod. 32:29;
Prov. 23:26;
1 Thess. 2:4

1. How should we present ourselves to God?

2. How does this 'please' God?

My Father, thank You for reminding me that the prayers which get answered are those that are in line with Your character. And what squares with Your character is always in my best interests. I am deeply grateful. Amen.

'A little of eternity'

FOR READING & MEDITATION – 2 CORINTHIANS 3:7–18

'And we all, who... contemplate the Lord's glory, are being transformed into his image' (v18, NIV 2011)

Today we begin by asking ourselves an intriguing question: why does Jesus, when laying down a pattern for prayer, say that our first consideration should be the glory and honour of God's name? Is this a device (as some have suggested) to appeal to the vanity of an egotistical God? Can it be that our loving heavenly Father wants us to give Him admiration and praise before He listens to our requests?

No, I do not believe so! God encourages us to focus on Him because He knows that in contemplating Him, we complete ourselves and bring all parts of our personality to health. To admire, appreciate, respect and venerate the character of God is to awaken ourselves to reality. Not to do so is to deprive ourselves and bring about a depletion of our humanness. We were designed for the worship and contemplation of God, and when, therefore, we stand before Him and contemplate His majesty and glory, the machinery of our inner being whirrs into activity, and our character takes on the lineaments of His character.

God, therefore, has our interests at heart more than His own when He asks us to honour Him. We 'hallow' His name, and our own name (character) is hallowed. We gaze at His character and our own character is made better for the gazing, or, as today's verse says, we are being transformed into His likeness. Someone put it this way: 'I just go quiet and empty in His presence, gaze at His glory and loveliness, and give myself time for His disposition to get through to mine.' 'Time for His disposition to get through' – that's great advice. Give God a little of your time, and He will give you a little of eternity.

FURTHER STUDY

2 Pet. 1;
Rom. 8:29;
Phil. 3:21;
1 John 3:2

1. How do we become partakers of the divine nature?

2. What are some of the characteristics of this nature?

Father, forgive me for the times I rush into Your presence intent only on getting my needs met. Slow me down and make me a more contemplative person. Then Your character can filter through to mine. In Jesus' name I pray. Amen.

Not just a 'Father'

FOR READING & MEDITATION – JOHN 17:1–11

'Holy Father, protect them by the power of your name' (v11)

We continue meditating on the phrase used by Jesus in the Lord's Prayer – 'hallowed be your name'. John Calvin, one of the great theologians of a past generation, said of this clause: 'That God's name should be hallowed is to say that God should have His own honour of which He is so worthy, so that [we] should never think or speak of Him without the greatest veneration.'

One of the things it is sad to see in the contemporary Christian Church is the way that some refer to God in terms that reduce Him to a kind of 'good buddy' relationship. They refer to the great God of creation as 'The Man Upstairs' or 'My Partner in the Sky'. When people talk about God in such low-level terms, they do Him an injustice. And it's not so much the terms, but the image of God that lies behind those terms which is the real problem.

FURTHER STUDY

Heb. 12:1–14;
Exod. 15:11;
1 Sam. 6:20;
Isa. 6:3;
Rev. 15:4

1. Where are we to look?

2. How do we become holy?

We must, of course, strike a balanced note on this issue, as Paul teaches that the Holy Spirit in our hearts prompts us to call God, not merely Father, but 'Daddy' (Rom. 8:15). Too much of the 'Daddy', however, can lead us, if we are not careful, into sloppy sentimentalism or into a casual approach to God. I believe this is why, after the phrase 'Our Father', Jesus introduces us to another aspect of God – hallowed, holy, reverenced be His name. It is right that we come to God as a child comes to their father but it is right also that we remember that our heavenly Father is a God of majestic holiness and unsullied purity. A.W. Tozer was right when he said, 'No religion has been greater than its idea of God.' Jesus put it into proper focus when He addressed God not only as Father, but Holy Father.

My Father and my God, help me gain a healthy and balanced view of Your person, so that while I enjoy the familiarity of Your Fatherhood, I am exceedingly conscious also of Your holiness. In Jesus' name. Amen.

A clear perspective

FOR READING & MEDITATION – PSALM 34:1–8

'Glorify the LORD with me: let us exalt his name together.' (v3)

We have seen over the past week that hallowing God's name does not mean having some kind of unhealthy preoccupation about pronouncing the word 'God' in hushed or reverential tones. It is rather hallowing all that God is: His qualities, His character and His attributes – all the things embodied in His name. When the psalmist in Psalm 102:15 said, 'The nations will fear the name of the LORD', did this mean they feared the letters in the word 'God' or 'Yahweh'? No, they feared the Lord God Himself.

At the risk of over-simplifying the opening clauses of the Lord's Prayer, what Jesus is teaching us is to come before the Father with this attitude: 'Our Father, who cares for us with true tenderness, and who has in heaven the supplies to meet our every need; may Your attributes, Your nature, Your character, Your reputation, Your person, Your whole being itself be hallowed.' This, then, is how prayer begins. Before we start asking for what we want from God, it's important that we gain a right perspective of the one who we come to in prayer.

FURTHER STUDY

Prov. 9:10;
Psa. 33:8;
34:9; 86:11

1. What is the beginning of wisdom?

2. What does it mean to fear the Lord?

Gregory of Nyssa prayed: 'May I become through Thy help blameless, just and holy. May I abstain from every evil, speak the truth and do justly. May I walk in the straight paths, sing with temperance, adorned with incorruption, beautiful through wisdom and prudence. May I meditate upon the things that are above and despise what is earthly, for a man can hallow God's name in no other way than by reflecting His character and bear witness to the fact that divine power is the cause of His goodness.' May we too echo this prayer, greeting each day with a fresh revelation of His name.

Gracious Father, I see that if I am to become close to You, then I need to get my priorities straight. Thank You for giving me a clear pattern to follow, and for reminding me that I need to hallow Your name. Thank You, Father. Amen.

'Your kingdom come'

FOR READING & MEDITATION – MATTHEW 6:25–34

'But seek first his kingdom... and all these things will be given to you as well.' (v33)

We turn now to examine the fourth phrase in the Lord's Prayer: 'Your kingdom come'. Jesus, after highlighting that the first consideration in prayer is to focus on God's character, puts as the next issue the establishing of God's kingdom. Our text today tells us: 'Seek first his kingdom and his righteousness, and all these things will be given to you as well.' If you seek something else first then your life will be off-balance.

A newspaper report told of a small town in Alaska where all the electric clocks were showing the wrong time. The fault, it appears, was in the local power plant. It failed to run with systematic regularity, and consequently all the electric clocks were 'out'. When your loyalty and primary concern is for something other than the kingdom of God, then everything in your life will be likely to be 'out' too.

FURTHER STUDY

Luke 9:51–62;
Matt. 5:3;
John 3:3;
James 2:5

1. What did Jesus teach about the kingdom?

2. What would Jesus say to His would-be followers?

Looking at Church history, one might argue that the Church has never really been gripped by the vision of the kingdom of God. There are notable exceptions, of course, but, by and large, the Church has missed its way in this matter. One theologian points out that when the Church drew up its creeds – the Apostles, the Athanasian, the Nicene – it mentioned the kingdom once in all three of them, and then only marginally. The Church will never move into the place that God has planned for it until it puts the kingdom where Jesus put it in this prayer – in a place of primary consideration and primary allegiance. J.I. Packer once said that to pray 'your kingdom come' is searching and demanding, for one must be ready to add, 'and start with me'.

Gracious Father, I begin to see that there is something here that demands my thought and attention, and I don't want to miss it. Prepare me in mind and spirit for what You want to teach me this week. In Jesus' name. Amen.

Help CWR today!

With your help, we can support even more people with our courses, continue to develop counselling training, create more resources for children, and supply prisoners with our publications. As a charity, a lot of the work we do is because of Partners who help support our work through regular prayer and donations.

If you can, we would love you to become a Partner from as little as 50p a day (£15 a month). Your regular gift will help us to:

· Develop Bible reading notes for future generations
· Send 60,000 vital resources to prisons in the UK and Australia
· Equip church leaders in the developing world with needed resources
· Create digital resources online for young adults to build tomorrow's Church
· Make new, fun, Bible-based resources for children

Without our Partners' support, we would be unable to do the work we do, so please consider supporting us and get in touch: partners@cwr.org.uk 01252 784709

As a Partner, you will receive quarterly newsletters keeping you up to date with our work and any exciting new developments. You will also be invited to attend Partners' Days, where you will hear from guest speakers and the CWR team, followed by a delicious meal.

The missing note

FOR READING & MEDITATION – MARK 1:9–28

'Jesus came to Galilee, preaching the gospel of the kingdom of God'
(v14, NKJV)

We said yesterday that the Christian Church down the centuries of Church history has never really been gripped by the vision of the kingdom of God. It has taught about it, of course, but it has never put the kingdom where Jesus put it in His pattern prayer, and given it the first consideration and the first allegiance.

'Your kingdom come' – three simple words in both English and Greek, yet they open to us something so vast that one approaches them like a small child standing on the seashore with a bucket in their hand wondering how to fit the vast ocean into their tiny pail! There is no way one can adequately and fully expound these words, but I hope I can whet your appetite over these next few days, and then you can spend the rest of your life exploring all that is beyond them.

In the second half of the twentieth century the Church woke up to the reality that there was a missing note in modern Christianity – the Holy Spirit. Gradually at first, and very tentatively, the Church rediscovered the Person of the Holy Spirit, and now there are comparatively few churches that have not been affected, to some degree at least, by His power and His presence. It seems strange, when we look back, that we could have remained content with a Holy Spirit-less type of Christianity. The same strange omission has taken place in regard to the kingdom of God. There are signs that the message is being emphasised in certain quarters and churches, but we are a long way from giving it the priority God demands. It's not surprising the Church has stumbled from issue to issue when its priorities are lost or pushed to the margins.

FURTHER STUDY

Dan. 2:36–44;
Mark 9:1;
1 Cor. 4:20;
John 18:36

1. What was the prophecy of Daniel?

2. What did Jesus say about His kingdom?

Gracious God, You who are always reaching out after me in love, and awakening me to new awareness and understanding, help me comprehend the truth of Your kingdom. In Jesus' name. Amen.

'Our God reigns'

FOR READING & MEDITATION – JOHN 18:28–40

'Jesus said, "My kingdom is not of this world."' (v36)

We have been saying over the past few days that although Jesus taught us to keep the vision of God's coming kingdom at the forefront of our prayers, the Church has possibly lost sight of the importance and understanding of this truth. The kingdom of God was the motif running through everything Jesus taught. I wonder, however, with all the valuable and helpful resources available to us today, how many of them give attention to the kingdom of God. Jesus made it the central note of His preaching and also His praying.

So, what does Jesus mean when He uses the word 'kingdom'? The word 'kingdom', *basileia* in the Greek, means 'rule' or 'reign'. The kingdom of God, then, is the rule or reign of God – His sovereignty – for which we are to pray. Jesus spoke of the kingdom as being in the present as well as in the future. In Luke 17:21 He said, 'the kingdom of God is within you'. Wherever there is a heart that is surrendered to the claims and authority of Jesus Christ, there the kingdom exists. But there is a day coming, says Jesus in Matthew 8:11, when both small and great will sit side by side in the kingdom, and realise that in God's order of things there are no favourites.

Scripture tells us also that God has a kingdom which is established in the heavens (Heb. 12:22–28), and the phrase we are studying – 'your kingdom come' – is a petition for God to let that kingdom extend to every area of the universe where His rule is resisted. We are thus introduced to another great purpose of prayer – transporting to all parts of the universe, across the bridge of prayer, the power that overcomes all sin, all rebellion and all evil.

FURTHER STUDY

Psa. 93:1–5;
47:8;
Exod. 15:18;
Micah 4:7;
Rom. 5:17

1. What does the psalmist conclude?

2. What is Paul's expectation?

Father, what can I say? When I see that You have given me the privilege of helping You usher in Your kingdom through my prayer, my heart is overwhelmed. What confidence You place in Your redeemed children. May we be worthy of it. Amen.

A world-view

FOR READING & MEDITATION – REVELATION 11:15–19

'The kingdom of the world has become the kingdom of our Lord and of his Christ, and he will reign for ever and ever.' (v15)

We continue meditating on the phrase 'your kingdom come'. Today we ask ourselves: why is it necessary to have at the forefront of our prayers a vision of the kingdom of God?

Philosophers have said that if we are to live effectively and securely in this world, then we must have a world-view of things – a cosmic framework in which to live, think and work. The Germans call it *Weltanschauung* – world-view. When we have a cosmic framework in which to think and work, then it gives a sense of validity and meaning to all we do. It makes us feel we are part of a universal purpose. Many modern thinkers believe that the reason why there is so much insecurity and anxiety prevalent in contemporary society is because there is a breakdown of that frame of reference. One writer says: 'Modern man is homesick. He is going on a hand-to-mouth existence day by day, and what he does and thinks does not seem to be related to the Whole. This has made life empty and jittery because it is insecure.'

The Chinese have a saying, 'in a broken nest there are no whole eggs', highlighting that if people want to be strong they must first build a strong country. The nest, the world in which we live and think and work, has been broken up by sin and, therefore, our central unity has gone. This can be seen even on a small scale when the home is broken. When the frameworks in which we were originally designed to live have been fractured it can leave us disconnected, confused and anxious. As a consequence, life breaks down. Jesus taught us to have a kingdom world-view. With our eyes focused on the kingdom, we know that at the heart of things there is utter security.

FURTHER STUDY

Psa. 24:1–10;
2 Chron. 20:6;
1 Tim. 1:17;
Rev. 19:6

1. What picture does the psalmist give us?

2. What is his exhortation?

Lord God, I am so grateful that I am not an orphan in this universe. I have a homeland, the kingdom of God. And because nothing can hinder the establishing of that kingdom, I have a peace that nothing can disturb. I am so grateful. Amen.

A position of strength

FOR READING & MEDITATION – 1 CORINTHIANS 15:12–28

'Then the end will come, when he hands over the kingdom to God the Father after he has destroyed all dominion' (v24)

Yesterday we referred to some philosophers and thinkers who said that if we are to live securely in this world then we must cultivate a world-view of things. We must understand the big picture. Is this why Jesus, when laying down a pattern for prayer, taught His disciples to focus on the big picture of the kingdom of God? It could well be, but whether it is or not, one thing is certain – when we start off in prayer gripped by the certainty of God's coming kingdom, our prayers are launched from a position of strength.

A sales leaflet once came in the post and on it were the words: 'Get the idea – and all else follows.' I thought to myself, when the idea is God's idea, the kingdom, then, indeed, all else follows. What if we were to begin our prayers, however, by focusing, not on the kingdom of God, but on the kingdoms of this world? We would receive very little motivation from such an action. The empires of this world come and go. Egypt came and went. Syria came and went. Babylon came and went. Greece came and went. Historians tell us that at least 21 former great civilisations are extinct. Earthly kingdoms go the way of all flesh – the corrupting consequence of sin, decay, distress and destruction is inevitable.

FURTHER STUDY

Psa. 115:1–18;
Phil. 2:10;
Heb. 1:8;
Rev. 11:15

1. How does the psalmist relate heaven and earth?

2. How can we help to bring the kingdom of heaven to earth?

The kingdom of God, unlike earthly kingdoms, is destined for success. Call it triumphalism if you like, but the eventual accomplishment of God's kingdom has more reliability about it than tomorrow's dawn. When our minds are permitted to focus on such a tremendous truth, it will not be long, believe me, before the heart leaps up in confident, trusting prayer.

Father, I think I get the idea. When I focus my mind on the glory of Your coming kingdom, then, against such a wonderful backdrop, my prayers take on a new confidence. Thank You, Father. Amen.

Eating our own words

FOR READING & MEDITATION – DANIEL 4:28–37

'His dominion is an eternal dominion; his kingdom endures from generation to generation.' (v34)

We have been studying over the past few days the phrase used by Jesus in the Lord's Prayer, 'your kingdom come'. This weekend, all over the UK and nations around the world, people are gathering to ask for God's kingdom to come as part of the National Prayer Weekend 2019. Today, churches who have been gathering prayer requests from their local communities are preparing to pray and petition God on their behalf. We said that one reason why Jesus taught us to focus on the coming kingdom was in order to help us get our spiritual bearings, and thus be better equipped and fortified when praying for other things. Just as mariners of the past had to get their bearings from the stars to be able to put into the right earthly port, so we have to get our eternal values straight before we begin to concentrate on temporal things. Oh that we could become so preoccupied with the kingdom of God that it would affect every part of our being, our thinking, our working and our praying.

Our own causes are valid only as they accord with the eternal cause of God. When I pray, 'your kingdom come', I am really praying, 'Lord, I pray that You will do whatever advances Your kingdom, whatever brings in Your rule and Your reign'. And, we might add, 'even though my own "cause" might have to be left aside.' What a prayer! What a challenge! No wonder the ancient Jewish Talmud said that 'the prayer in which there is no mention of the kingdom of God is no prayer at all.' It's only when we get the kingdom values straight that we can pray this prayer with assurance.

FURTHER STUDY

Mark 4:30–41;
Isa. 9:7;
Dan. 7:13–14;
Luke 1:32–33

1. How would you define 'the kingdom'?

2. To what did Jesus liken the kingdom?

Father, this weekend I want to join my prayers with those who are praying for Your kingdom to come in their communities, and that my friends and neighbours might know Your loving care. In Jesus' name I pray. Amen.

For more information about the National Prayer Weekend, visit national-prayer-weekend.com

'Your will be done'

FOR READING & MEDITATION – PSALM 103:1–22

'Praise the LORD, you his angels, you mighty ones who do his bidding'
(v20)

On this second day of the National Prayer Weekend, we come today to the fifth clause, or petition as it is sometimes called, in Jesus' pattern for praying: 'your will be done, on earth as it is in heaven'. However, if we are to know how God's will is to be done on earth, then we need to know how it is done in heaven. We ask ourselves, therefore: how is the will of God followed by the myriads of angels and other celestial beings who inhabit eternity?

First, it is followed unquestioningly because they know and understand His love and His true character. If only we could fully grasp and comprehend God's true nature and His love, we too would have no hesitation in carrying out His will. Second, it is done speedily. Once asked, the angels move promptly to carry out His plans. Then contentedly wait for the next command so they can hurry to accomplish it. How slow and sluggish are we, His earthly servants, by comparison. Third, it is done completely. The angels carry out His bidding down to the tiniest detail. There are no alternatives, no omissions, no modifications to the divine orders. The will of God is done in fullest detail.

A little girl, seven years of age, asked me once, 'Does an angel have a will?' I said, 'I think so.' 'Then how many wills are there in heaven?' she asked. 'Oh,' I said, 'there must be millions.' 'Wrong,' she said. 'There is only one. There were two once, but one got kicked out. Now God's will has full control.' I smiled at such clarity of thought from a seven-year-old. May the day soon dawn when the will of God is done on earth as it is done in heaven – unquestioningly, speedily and completely.

FURTHER STUDY

Isa. 14:12–15;
Neh. 9:6;
Luke 10:18

1. Why was the 'morning star' ('Lucifer' in NKJV) cast out of heaven?

2. What phrase occurs five times?

Lord God, may Your will be done in my life as it is in heaven. Help me to be as responsive to Your voice as the angels of heaven. In Jesus' name. Amen.

God's totalitarianism

FOR READING & MEDITATION – 1 CORINTHIANS 15:24–28

'the Son himself will be made subject to him who put everything under him, so that God may be all in all.' (v28)

We continue our meditations on the question: how is God's will done in heaven? We considered yesterday that the angels respond to the will of God with unquestioning obedience and perform His will with the utmost readiness and willingness. It's because they are known and know the full extent of God's love for them. Heaven has been described by some as a totalitarian society. However, in God there is no coercion or manipulation.

We are rather afraid of that word here on earth, as it brings to mind oppressive regimes where individualism is discouraged or repressed, sometimes in a most brutal manner. We may recognise that the word does have negative connotations because of this but, make no mistake about it, heaven is a totalitarian community. However, there is a profound difference. When you follow the will of God fully and completely, you find perfect freedom. When you come under other totalitarian systems, you find utter bondage, for they are not in line with the way you were designed to live.

FURTHER STUDY

Heb. 10:1–12;
John 14:31;
15:10;
Rom. 5:19

1. What was Christ's example?

2. What was His challenge?

As the stomach and poison are incompatible, so your life and 'other-than-the-will-of-God' ways are not made for each other and also result in pain and death. However, just as the stomach thrives on good wholesome food, and because the two are made for each other they bring health and life, so the will of God and your innermost being are made for each other, and when brought together produce health, life, joyous release and fulfilment. Let's again join with others around the nations and pray that our local communities, streets and neighbours will have their spiritual eyes opened to God's true nature and character, sowing the seeds for the next great move of God.

Lord God, drive this truth deep into my spirit, that it is only as I give myself to Your reign that I truly realise myself. Your will is my release. Not just for me, but those around me also. May Your will be done today in my town, my street and my life. Amen.

'Made for each other'

FOR READING & MEDITATION – HOSEA 8:1–14

'I wrote for them... my law, but they regarded them as something alien.' (v12)

We saw yesterday that where God's will is followed, and followed completely, then that society could be perceived as totalitarian. We may dislike the word because of its negative connotations, but we cannot get away from the fact that God's way, and His will for humankind, is best. However, as we said, it is a regime with a profound difference. When we obey completely the will of men, we often find manipulation, coercion and power plays. When we obey completely the will of God, we find nothing but freedom – perfect freedom.

There are many in this universe who think like Ephraim, of whom God complained: 'I wrote for them the many things of my law, but they regarded them as something alien' (v12). Ephraim felt that God's laws were something alien. But the will of God and the human will are not alien. They were made for each other. The expression is inadequate, but it is the best way I know of explaining the fact that my life works best when I live and behave in accordance with His will.

If only we would fully understand and grasp this basic axiom: my will and God's will are not alien. When I find His will, I find my own. I am fulfilled when I make Him my centre, I am frustrated when I make myself the centre. And if you are afraid that this depletes you as a person or makes you into a cipher by subduing your individuality, then your fear is quite groundless. You are really at your best only when you are walking in the will of God. Then all parts of your personality are drawn to health, vitality and fulfilment. Enoch understood that walking in God's will is best and 'he was commended as one who pleased God' (Heb. 11:5).

FURTHER STUDY

Psa. 40:1–8; 143:10; Matt. 12:50; Eph. 6:6

1. What is the psalmist's request?

2. What is the testimony of the psalmist?

God my Father, thank You for reminding me that Your will and my will were made for each other. When my will and Yours coincide, then I live. When they clash, I do not live. Lord, I want to live. Amen.

Forced to face reality

FOR READING & MEDITATION – ROMANS 12:1–8

'offer your bodies as living sacrifices... be transformed by the renewing of your mind.' (vv1–2)

We continue meditating on the phrase: 'your will be done on earth as it is in heaven'. Whenever we pray, we are to pray in accordance with God's will. One Greek scholar says that these words can be paraphrased in this way: 'Your will, whatever You wish to happen, let it happen – as in heaven so in earth.' In other words, 'God, do what You want.' It's not easy to pray this way. If anyone thinks it is, then it is probably because they have never really sounded the depths of self-interest within their own hearts.

FURTHER STUDY

1 John 5:1–15;
James 4:13–17;
1 John 2:17

1. What is the confidence we have?

2. What ought we to say?

It's hard sometimes to pray 'your will be done' when we know that if God has His way, we will not get our way. Has that ever happened to you? The basic reason for this conflict is due to the major problem of the human heart – self-centredness. Paul, when describing a self-centred life and its results in Romans 6:21, ends by asking this question: 'What did you get out of it? Nothing you're proud of now. Where did it get you? A dead end' (*The Message*). The end was zero. That is the inevitable end of a self-centred life – nothing. The major thing that stands in the way of God performing His will in our lives utterly and completely is just that – self-centredness.

Did Jesus know that when His disciples prayed this prayer, 'your will be done', it would sometimes produce a conflict within them? In my own mind, I am sure He did. He nevertheless framed the statement in the way He did because He knew, as we now do, that if we are to grow spiritually, then we must face up to the question: whose will comes first – mine or God's? Am I willing to say, 'God, do what You want'? That is the bottom line in prayer.

Gracious Father, I am grateful for the gentle and loving way You are showing me the obstacles in my life. Give me the attitude that puts Your will first and my will second. For Jesus' sake. Amen.

Louder than 'Amen'

FOR READING & MEDITATION – PSALM 40:1–8

'I desire to do your will, O my God; your law is within my heart.' (v8)

We saw yesterday that to pray the words 'your will be done' sometimes creates a conflict in us, particularly at such times when we know that God's will is the opposite of what we ourselves want. We, then, must consider whose will is to have precedence – ours or God's.

There are some Christians who pray 'your will be done', but they do it with a wrong attitude – an attitude of lingering resentment. They believe that they cannot escape the inevitable, and they are in danger of becoming bitter about it. When they say the words 'your will be done', they are almost said through clenched teeth. Other people say the words, not necessarily out of resentment, but with an attitude of passive resignation. They say the words 'your will be done', but what they mean is something like this: 'Lord, I'm not very happy about the way things are turning out, but I suppose You know best. So I'll go along with it and try my best to believe it's for the best.'

Our attitude to the will of God, and the goal for which we can aim, is one of peace and contentment. Not always easy to arrive at such an attitude, I know, but nevertheless we have it before us as the desired end. David, as we read today, prayed that way. Interestingly these words also apply to Jesus who delighted to do God's will (see Heb. 10:5–11). If we can cultivate that attitude as the normal and characteristic reaction to everything that happens around us – sorrow, disappointment, disillusionment, frustration, disaster, loss, bereavement – then such a spirit is more than a match for anything. As someone has said: 'The Hallelujah of triumph is louder than the Amen of resignation.'

FURTHER STUDY

Psa. 100:1–5;
1 John 5:30;
Eph. 6:6;
Heb. 13:21

1. What is the psalmist's exhortation?

2. What should be our heart attitude?

Father God, help me drop my anchor into the depths of Your eternal love, and ride out all storms in the assurance that You are willing my highest good. Help me to accept it – peaceably. Amen.

'On' or 'in'

FOR READING & MEDITATION – ROMANS 8:18–25

'We know that the whole creation has been groaning as in the pains of childbirth right up to the present time.' (v22)

We continue meditating on the phrase: 'your will be done, on earth as it is in heaven'.

Today we ask ourselves: what does Jesus mean by the term 'on earth'? Theologians have argued for centuries over the preposition used here. Some say it should be 'in' earth, and others say it should be 'on' earth. I think that the word 'on' is the truer translation, but I take the point that some theologians make when they say: 'The phrase "in earth" more nearly expresses the meaning than "on earth" because God's ultimate will is destined to rule not only over the minds of men, but over the disharmony and dissolution that is inherent in planet earth.'

FURTHER STUDY

Psa. 8:1–9;
Gen. 1:26

1. What was God's original purpose?

2. How did Jesus illustrate this?

Paul put his finger on this issue when, speaking by the Holy Spirit in the passage before us today, he says, 'the whole creation has been groaning'. Who can doubt it? Despite the beauty of this glorious creation, everything that lives is subject to degeneration, disease and decay. Life seems strangely poisoned near the fount. The lady who wrote the hymn *All things bright and beautiful* was only looking at some aspects of creation. She was being selective. She wasn't seeing nature 'whole'. But Paul did! If you place your ear to the ground (metaphorically speaking, of course), you will hear the groan of a creation that is crying out to be delivered from the effects of sin. But be assured of this – there is a day coming when the will of God will impose itself, not only 'on' the earth, but 'in' the earth, and 'in keeping with his promise' He will restore this sin-affected planet to its original beauty and majesty by bringing in 'a new heaven and a new earth, the home of righteousness' (2 Pet. 3:13).

Father, You originally made the earth as You made me – to reflect Your eternal glory. But sin has spoiled both. I look forward to that day when You will bring in 'a new heaven and a new earth'. Thank You, Father. Amen.

Doing His will – now

FOR READING & MEDITATION – PHILIPPIANS 2:1–16

'for it is God who works in you to will and the act according to his good purpose.' (v13)

We said yesterday that theologians are divided over the issue of whether the statement of Jesus should be translated 'in earth' or 'on earth'. We decided to examine both prepositions and today we now look at the words 'on earth'.

Most commentators believe the phrase has reference to the world of human beings who have their home on this earth. In other words – us. Fantastic as it may sound, a day will dawn when this earth will be renewed and peopled with those who will do the will of God, not with resentment or resignation, but with a wholeheartedness. That day may not be as far distant as we may think, so let's give ourselves in prayer, and willingly become involved in bringing our lives in line with His will. One thing is sure – the more you and I conform to His will, the more quickly can His purposes for this earth be realised.

I have quoted before the famous words of John Wesley who said, 'God does nothing redemptively in this world except by prayer.' Can you see what he is saying? Although the Bible clearly tells us that God 'works out everything in conformity with the purpose of his will' (Eph. 1:11), in some way that purpose of God for the future will have to cross the bridge of prayer. This raises the question: how committed are you and I to doing the will of God? Are we hindering or are we promoting the interests of His future kingdom? It is vital that we Christians, both individually and corporately, focus our prayers on this issue in faith and trust, remembering as we do so that the more in tune we are to the divine will, the more speedily will His purposes come to pass for the world.

FURTHER STUDY

Matt. 3;
John 8:29;
1 Thess. 4:1;
Heb. 13:16

1. What was the pronouncement from heaven?

2. Could this be said of your life?

Father, in the light of this challenge today, I want to pray, 'your will be done on earth *in me* as it is done in heaven'. Grant it, I pray, for the honour and glory of Your peerless name. Amen.

These Three Things:
Security, Self-worth and Significance

Who am I? What am I here for? Do I matter?

These are questions so many of us are asking – no matter our age or the culture we live in.

The Bible describes us all as 'thirsty' – thirsty for purpose, value and love in any way we can experience, whether through our roles in the workplace, church or home; through countless activities and achievements; or through our relationships with other people. Yet it was Jesus who said that it was through Him that we can know life in all its fullness, and throughout Scripture we read of being made in God's image, created to have our deepest longings met in God.

But how do we actively live this out? How do we learn to trust God when problems arise, things don't go to plan, we feel anxious, angry or disappointed in life?

Based on the seminal work of Selwyn Hughes, presented in his book *Christ Empowered Living*, Mick Brooks now offers a fresh approach to how we can deepen our dependence on God to meet our need for security, self-worth and significance.

These 3 things

This new resource takes an accessible approach to understanding the key elements of our personalities; the strategies we follow, thinking we know best how to make life work; and ways in which we can learn to rethink how to have our needs met and function well – even when life becomes a struggle.

The book: 42 days to help you lean into God every day and discover how to find your security, self-worth and significance in God

The group resource: Free online videos and discussion starters to help you fully unpack this vital, life-transforming teaching

The church programme: Sermon outlines and PowerPoint templates to help your whole church benefit in journeying through *These Three Things* together

Provisional cover

Available from October

For prices and further information, visit **cwr.org.uk/t3t** or use the order form at the back of these notes.

ISBN: 978-1-78259-828-2

A change of focus

FOR READING & MEDITATION – 1 TIMOTHY 2:1–7
'I urge, then, first of all, that... thanksgiving be made' (v1)

The Lord's Prayer falls naturally into two sections: the first division focusing upon God, and the second division focusing on ourselves. We come now to the second part of the prayer, the part which has to do with our physical, psychological and spiritual needs. This natural division once again reinforces the truth we have been seeing, that it is when God is given His rightful place that we can have the proper perspective towards ourselves. Jesus begins this part of the prayer by encouraging us to petition God for our physical needs: 'Give us today our daily bread'.

FURTHER STUDY

Luke 17:11–19;
Deut. 8:10;
Psa. 100:4;
Col. 1:12

1. How did the lepers show ingratitude?

2. What can you give God thanks for today?

Some Christians believe that it is inappropriate for many of us who live in the Western world to give expression to these words because, they say, our problem is not so much where do we get the next meal, but how do we keep from eating the next meal! In an overfed, overweight society, so they say, our prayer ought to be: 'Lord, teach us self-discipline, and prevent us from eating more than we need.'

At first glance, the phrase which Jesus used – 'Give us today our daily bread' – does seem somewhat inappropriate, at least for those of us who live in a place of plenty. This prayer might be better suited to those who often face the reality of going without. However, to take that view is to misunderstand the deep truth which Jesus wants us to absorb. He invites us to pray, 'Give us today our daily bread', because when we say these words with sincerity and meaning, we build for ourselves a barrier against ingratitude. All that comes from God is not be taken for granted, but with recognition and gratitude.

Lord Jesus, every statement of Yours is filled with light and meaning. Show me the truth behind the words 'Give us today our daily bread'. You have shown me that I need to be thankful, but help me understand more. In Your name I pray. Amen.

We need to tell Him

FOR READING & MEDITATION – PHILIPPIANS 4:4–9

*'Do not be anxious about anything, but in everything...
with thanksgiving, present your requests to God.' (v6)*

We ended yesterday by saying that one of the reasons why Jesus taught us to pray – 'Give us today our daily bread' – was because He wanted to build in us a barrier against ingratitude.

Before we enlarge on that point, permit me to ask you a personal question: do you pray daily for your physical needs? Do you ask God daily for things like food, shelter and the other physical necessities of life? I must confess that when I asked myself that question before writing this page, I had to admit that I did not. As a result I made a decision to apply myself to this part of the Lord's Prayer with greater sincerity and meaning.

Of course, some people argue that because Jesus said, 'Your Father knows what you need before you ask him' (Matt. 6:8), then it is pointless to inform God of our physical needs. He knows them already – so they say. Here we touch the central value of prayer. Prayer is not something by which we inform God of our needs, and thus influence Him to give things to us. Prayer is designed to influence us – it is we who are in need of this kind of prayer, not God. Of course God knows what we are in need of, but He also knows that unless we come face to face daily with the truth that we are creatures of need, then we can soon develop a spirit of independence, and withdraw ourselves from close contact and fellowship with Him. Prayer, then, is something we need to help us to develop a dependent trust in our heavenly Father. God may not need to be told, but we need to tell Him. That's the point. And unless we grasp it, we can miss one of the primary purposes of prayer – learning to trust God to supply all our needs.

FURTHER STUDY

Matt. 6:19–34;
Psa. 37:5;
118:8; 125:1

1. What should be our attitude to worldly cares?

2. What should be our first priority?

Father, thank You for showing me that prayer is not begging for blessings. It is helping me to grow closer to You. I pray that my attitude towards You will change to one of more reliance on Your care for me. Thank You, Father. Amen.

Give thanks to the Lord

FOR READING & MEDITATION – PSALM 92:1–8

'It is good to praise the Lord' (v1)

We continue our thoughts from yesterday when we ended by saying that we pray, not because God has a need to know our circumstances, but because we have a need to tell Him about them and that we need to learn to trust God to supply our needs. To understand the truth of this statement we ask ourselves: what happens when we neglect to pray for our daily needs and thank God for providing them? If we are honest about it, and examine our lives over a period of time, we will discover subtle changes taking place in our feelings and in our thinking. When we neglect to pray for our needs we will begin to take the blessings of life for granted and, gradually, without at first realising it, we will succumb to the senseless notion that we can provide for the necessities of life, and that we are capable of managing our own affairs without any help from God.

When we think that way, it is not long before pride steps in and a kind of spiritual blindness settles upon us which blocks our vision in relation to God, ourselves and others. We need, therefore, to constantly remind ourselves that everything we have comes from His hand and that, at any moment, in this chaotic and corrupt world, things could change. We can build a barricade against the damaging consequences of ingratitude by praying daily with thankfulness for our needs, remembering, as the poet said:

FURTHER STUDY

1 Kings 17;
Psa. 23:5;
Isa. 41:10;
Mal. 3:10

1. How did God test Elijah's faith?
2. How did he respond?

> *'Back of the bread is the snowy flour,*
> *And back of the flour, the mill,*
> *And back of the mill is the field of wheat,*
> *The rain, and the Father's will.'*

Father, teach me the art of continual thankfulness, and help me never to become bored with acknowledging Your grace and goodness, otherwise life will begin to disintegrate. Help me, Lord Jesus. Amen.

'They shall be satisfied'

FOR READING & MEDITATION – PSALM 37:1–19

'in the days of famine they shall be satisfied.' (v19, NKJV)

We have been seeing over the past few days that one reason Jesus directs us to ask God for our daily bread is not because God has a need to know, but because we have a need to ask. It does us good to ask, for by asking we increase the awareness of our dependency upon God and build a defence against the insidiousness of ingratitude.

I find it greatly encouraging that the God of creation, who is infinitely holy, and who holds the universe in His hand, cares that my physical needs are met. This implies that God regards our bodies as important. He designed them and engineered them and is interested in the way they function. Some Christians regard it as 'unspiritual' to pray about the needs of the body but, as Jesus highlights, this is really where our personal petitions begin. As the rest of Matthew chapter 6 goes on to show, Jesus keeps His disciples focused on His priorities by encouraging us to invest in heaven (vv19–21), and not to worry about daily needs but rather 'seek first his kingdom and his righteousness' (v33). Nevertheless when we pray in this petition to 'Give us today our daily bread' God is showing us that our physical needs are important too.

FURTHER STUDY

John 6:1–15;
Psa. 37:25;
Joel 2:24;
Luke 6:38

1. What was the disciples' attitude?

2. How did Jesus show His dependence on God?

Most of the promises in the Bible have to do with spiritual truth, but never to the exclusion of the physical. How much spiritual use would we be to our heavenly Father if He didn't meet our basic physical needs? This is why I do not fear the future. However men might mismanage the resources which God has placed in the earth, I have confidence in the truth of the verse before us today: 'in the days of famine they shall be satisfied.'

Father, help me not to get bogged down in wrong attitudes about the physical factors of my life, for they are a part of me. Teach me to live, physically and spiritually, in dependence on You. In Jesus' name. Amen.

God's storehouse

FOR READING & MEDITATION – GENESIS 1:29–31

'Then God said, "I give you every seed-bearing plant... and every tree that has fruit with seed in it. They will be yours for food."' (v29)

The question being considered from several different angles this week is this: do we thank God daily for His provision for the physical necessities of life? Some might respond to this by saying: 'But we never eat a meal without saying grace or giving thanks.' Ah, but are you really thankful? Do you look up into your Father's face every day, acknowledging that He is the source of everything, and give Him thanks?

The term bread is regarded by most Bible teachers as a broad term for food. Just think for a moment what God has provided in the way of nourishment for His children. He has provided food in the grains of wheat, barley and so on, and, according to Genesis 43:11 and Numbers 11:5, He has provided nuts, vegetables, melons, and a whole host of other things. Keep looking in God's storehouse and you will find food plants such as grapes, raisins, olives and apples. In addition to this, there is livestock, such as oxen, sheep and goats, as well as different kinds of fowl. Then there are fish, and according to Leviticus chapter 11, even four types of insects!

How diverse and plentiful is His provision. One has only to turn to Psalm 104 to see how the psalmist praises God for all His works of creation and providence in providing for all His creation.

Not to recognise that is indeed the height of thoughtlessness. As the old hymn so aptly puts it:

'Its streams the whole creation reach
So plenteous is the store.
Enough for all, enough for each,
Enough for evermore.'

FURTHER STUDY

Exod. 16;
Gen. 9:3;
Psa. 104:14;
136:25;
Matt. 6:26

1. What three things did God provide for the children of Israel?

2. What are some of the things God has provided for you?

Father, something is being burned into my consciousness – You are a bountiful and magnanimous God. Keep me awake and alert, day after day, to Your loving concern for my physical and spiritual care. Amen.

Recipients of providence

FOR READING & MEDITATION – JAMES 1:12–18

'Every good and perfect gift is from above, coming down from the Father' (v17)

We continue meditating on the ability of God to meet the physical needs of the human race. The thought of it staggered one scientist: 'On this earth,' he said, 'with its diameter of 7,800 miles – a trifle too large to play with! – God is keeping in His charge some four billion black-haired or light-haired, two-legged vertebrate animals. What a family – yet He feeds them all.'

There are many difficulties and problems facing us today in relation to economy, but the issue is not really that the earth cannot provide enough food. If there is a failure, it is a failure of distribution, not a failure in production. The food is there, but it is not properly managed or apportioned. The once Prime Minister of India, Mrs Gandhi, said that there are enough resources in India to feed that nation entirely and then export two-thirds of what it produces.

It's simply not correct to blame God for the thousands of people who may die of starvation each year. The fault is not in Him, but in us. God has given us His gracious promise: 'As long as the earth endures, seedtime and harvest, cold and heat, summer and winter, day and night will never cease' (Gen. 8:22). As Isaac Watts puts it in his grand old hymn:

> 'Thy providence is kind and large,
> Both man and beast Thy bounty share;
> The whole creation is Thy charge,
> But saints are Thy peculiar care.'

Is it not so? Yet how slow we are to pause and reflect that we are, in fact, literally the recipients of providence!

FURTHER STUDY

James 5;1–6;
Exod. 23:25;
Psa. 81:16;
Isa. 30:23

1. What does James say about selfish living?

2. What are we to live in the light of?

Father, when I think of Your bountiful goodness and grace, I find it difficult to express my feelings. I echo the psalmist's words: 'You open your hand and satisfy the desires of every living thing.' For that I am always grateful. Amen.

No lack of resources

FOR READING & MEDITATION – PSALM 33:1–22

'the eyes of the LORD are on those who fear him, on those whose hope is in his unfailing love' (v18)

Let us spend one more day in considering the bountiful provision of our great creator. A modern writer tells how once he asked an old man how he managed to live alone in a single cottage, miles from anywhere. The old man answered cheerfully that he enjoyed it since, as he explained, 'Providence is my next-door neighbour'.

Despite what many politicians and scientists tell us, the problems of this earth are not physical but spiritual. It is not over-population that requires our attention, but spiritual immaturity. If people came into a knowledge of Jesus as their Lord and Saviour, then they would gain new insights and be perceptive on how to use the earth's resources in the right manner. One writer has suggested that only 15% of the arable land on the globe is being farmed and only half of that every year. Such a figure reflects how humanity mismanages much of the earth's resources when it has potential to feed the whole population of the world. It goes without saying, of course, that although God supplies the basic necessities, man has to put some effort into harvesting them; but, I say again, our problem is not lack of resources, nor too many people – it is our lack of dependency upon God.

FURTHER STUDY

James 2;
Rom. 12:11;
Prov. 13:11;
2 Thess. 3:10

1. How does James relate faith and works?

2. What is Paul's exhortation?

Paul in 1 Timothy 4:3 says that God has created all food 'to be received with thanksgiving by those who believe and who know the truth'. Can you see what this verse is saying? God has provided an incredible abundance of food that we might express our thanks to Him. The rest of the world indulges with little thought. Let's make sure that not one day passes without this prayer meaningfully crossing our lips: 'Give us today our daily bread.'

Heavenly Father, now that I understand the significance of Your words, 'Give us today our daily bread', help me, every time I say them, to make them, not just a recitation, but a realisation. In Jesus' name. Amen.

Follow the pattern

FOR READING & MEDITATION – PSALM 32:1–11

'Blessed is he whose transgressions are forgiven' (v1)

We turn now to consider the next petition of that part of the Lord's Prayer that focuses on us: 'And forgive us our trespasses, as we forgive those who trespass against us'. I have used this rendering of this part of the Lord's Prayer because it uses the word 'trespasses' in preference to the word 'debts'. In our modern society the word 'debt' has come to have a monetary significance and, by reason of this, has become somewhat narrowed. The word 'trespass' has a wider significance and implies an offence done against another – an intrusion into someone's rights.

This second section of Jesus' pattern of prayer takes in every level of human life: the physical, the psychological and the spiritual. 'Give us today' refers to the physical part of life. 'Forgive us our trespasses' has to do with the psychological part of life (the emotions, the thoughts and the will), and 'lead us not into temptation' has to do with the spiritual part of life.

With characteristic accuracy, Jesus focuses on the paramount need in human life. If we understand the Lord's Prayer correctly, there is really nothing more to be said when we come to this matter of prayer. This does not mean, of course, that prayer has to be limited to these statements of Jesus, but it does mean that the issues He deals with, although we can expand upon them, cover the entire range of human need, and are the pattern for all adequate and effective praying. When we fail to address the issues raised in Jesus' pattern of prayer, expanding on them in our own words, we deny ourselves the true resources that lie in prayer. Follow the pattern and you find the power.

FURTHER STUDY

Eph. 1:7; 3:14–21; Phil. 4:19; Rom. 2:4

1. What is Paul's desire for the Ephesians?

2. What is the 'inner man'?

Lord God, in a world torn and fragmented, I need guidance as to how to bring Your help into my life. In this matchless model of prayer, You have given it to me. Help me follow it and discover Your strength. In Jesus' name. Amen.

The biggest single problem

FOR READING & MEDITATION – PSALM 51:1–17

'Create in me a pure heart, O God, and renew a steadfast spirit within me.... Save me from bloodguilt, O God' (vv10,14)

Today we begin by asking ourselves a pointed question: what is the biggest single problem that faces us in human life? Some would say ill-health; others, lack of money; still others, uncertainty about the future, or fear of dying. My own view is that the biggest single problem with which human beings have to grapple is the problem of guilt. A sense of guilt is the most powerfully destructive force in the personality. We cannot live with guilt (that is, *truly* live).

When I was a young Christian, I heard some great preaching in my native Wales, most of which focused on how God was able to release us from the guilt of inbred sin. Nowadays, apart from a few exceptions, that message is hardly heard in the pulpits of the Principality, or for that matter, in many other pulpits elsewhere. The emphasis on a person's guilt before a holy God seems to have little impact on contemporary society and so was discarded. However, that guilt cannot be silenced, it has to come out – and it has resurfaced through the science of psychology. Someone said that the point at which psychology and religion meet is at the point of guilt. Christianity and the social sciences underline what the human heart knows so well – it cannot live comfortably with guilt.

FURTHER STUDY

John 8:1–11;
Psa. 40:12;
38:4; 73:21

1. What made the Pharisees leave?

2. How did Jesus respond to the woman?

In this simple prayer of Jesus, however, we have an adequate answer: 'Forgive us our trespasses, as we forgive those who trespass against us.' If we have fully accepted the forgiveness of God, and we know that our sins have been forgiven, then the result is a pervading sense of peace. The human heart cannot be put off by subterfuge: it needs reconciliation, forgiveness, assurance.

God my Father, I see that within the ways of humanity, You have a way – a way that is written into the nature of reality. And that way is a way of forgiveness. May I ever walk in it. Amen.

Wellbeing Groups

Join the movement to set up safe and supportive communities for people to grow and flourish

CWR is excited to be partnering with Kintsugi Hope in creating a structured yet very flexible 12-week course to help people accept themselves, understand their value and worth, and grow towards a more resilient future.

Each week includes group and individual activities and will be run by a group leader who has been specially trained to host and guide the group – whether it's held in a church, a coffee shop, a workplace, or their existing small group.

Over the 12 weeks, the course will cover topics such as anxiety, depression, anger, shame, disappointment, perfectionism, self-acceptance and healthy relationships. Each week, the content can be tailor-made to the needs of the group in positive, encouraging, non-threatening and non-judgmental ways.

If you would like to know more about how you can be trained to run groups in your church or community, then visit **kintsugihope.com** for more information or for an application pack.

(Please note – all applicants for training must be supported/endorsed by their local church, even if the groups will not be run within the church.)

God's thorn hedges

FOR READING & MEDITATION – ROMANS 3:21–31

'in his forbearance he had left the sins committed beforehand unpunished' (v25)

We continue our discussion on the question of guilt and our need to be forgiven. There are some psychiatrists who take the attitude that guilt, being dangerous to the personality, must be dealt with by persuading their clients that there is no basis for their guilt feelings, that conscience and the moral universe are manmade concepts, and must be eliminated. There is nothing, they say, to feel guilty about, so, as some put it, 'let bygones be bygones and wave goodbye to guilt'.

It must be acknowledged that some ideas regarding guilt have to be dealt with in that way, for some guilt is false and needlessly torments many sincere people. However, I am not talking here about false guilt, I am talking about real guilt – the guilt that the human heart carries because it has acted independently of God. You cannot get rid of that by waving your hand and saying, 'let bygones be bygones.' Nor can you get away from sin by joking about it. Oscar Wilde said: 'The only way to get rid of a temptation is to yield to it.' But you do not get rid of temptation by yielding to it. It becomes an act, and then a habit and then part of you.

FURTHER STUDY

Psa. 32:1–11;
Acts 2:37;
Ezra 9:6;
John 16:8

1. What was the result of guilt?

2. What did confession produce?

No, we are hedged in – thorn hedges on either side. The only open door is the mercy of God. And these thorn hedges are His provision, too. These thorns act, in some ways like lights on the path to an emergency exit, directing us towards the place of safety and escape. I say again, guilt cannot be banished by subterfuge. God can truly redeem our insistence on living our lives independently from Him but it is only at the cross of Calvary where we can find true freedom and forgiveness and reconciliation.

Lord God, only You can help me with real guilt. I bring my guilty heart to You for cleansing, forgiveness and reconciliation. In Jesus' name. Amen.

Nothing hidden

FOR READING & MEDITATION – LUKE 12:1–7

'There is nothing concealed that will not be disclosed, or hidden that will not be made known.' (v2)

We continue meditating on the problem of guilt, and our need for divine forgiveness. In today's text Jesus, in warning His disciples about the hypocrisy of the Pharisees, shows us that no one gets away with anything in this universe. *The Message* puts it like this: 'You can't keep your true self hidden forever; before long you'll be exposed.' It will at some point be 'disclosed', either voluntarily, and forgiveness sought, or it will be disclosed as an inner conflict or turmoil. In any case, it is 'disclosed'.

The young doctor in A.J. Cronin's book *The Citadel* found his inner problems were disclosed. When politics defeated his proposed health measures in a Welsh mining town, he sold his standards for money. After his wife's tragic death, he found in her handbag snapshots of himself taken during his crusading days. It reminded him of the man he might have been. He knew his pain was deserved and he shouted at himself in a drunken stupor: 'You thought you could get away with it. You thought you were getting away with it. But… you weren't.'

We cannot get away with guilt, either by waving goodbye to it or by bottling it up within you. It reveals itself in one way or another in our personalities. Lady Macbeth, in Shakespeare's play, said: 'What, will these hands ne'er be clean? Here's the smell of the blood still. All the perfumes of Arabia will not sweeten this little hand.' Only the blood of Jesus can erase the stain of guilt upon the human heart (see 1 John 1:7–10). When we pray, 'Forgive us our trespasses', we are asking for the reality that God promises to everyone who asks of Him. And the only way we can fail to experience it, is simply not to ask.

FURTHER STUDY

Dan. 5;
Gen. 3:8;
42:21;
Heb. 9:14

1. Why did Belshazzar call for Daniel?

2. What was Daniel's pronouncement?

Father, I am so grateful that when I confess my sins, they are fully and freely forgiven at a stroke. There is no period of probation or parole. I ask – and it is done. What clemency! Thank You, dear Father. Amen.

The divine example

FOR READING & MEDITATION – LUKE 23:32–43

'Jesus said, "Father, forgive them, for they do not know what they are doing."' (v34)

W e have been meditating on the need for divine forgiveness, but it is time now to focus on the truth that Jesus adds a condition to this statement. He says that we can only ask God to forgive us our trespasses when we are willing to forgive those who have trespassed against us. Thomas Watson put it like this: 'Our forgiving others is not a cause of God's forgiving us, but it is a condition without which he will not forgive us.'

Does this mean that before we become followers of Jesus, and have our sins forgiven, we have to search our hearts in order to make sure that we hold no bitterness or resentment against anyone? No. There is nothing in the Scripture that states that a non-Christian receives forgiveness from God on the basis of claiming to forgive everyone else. Jesus is referring here, so I believe, to those who are His followers. They have been forgiven for their sins, but now Jesus reveals 'how it is in heaven'; how to live as God intended. How, when we get off track, do we deal with the issues that arise in our personalities?

Paul says: 'In him we have redemption through his blood, the forgiveness of our trespasses, according to the riches of his grace' (Eph. 1:7, ESV). Grace – that's the basis of our forgiveness when we first come to Christ. But although we have received that forgiveness, we can never fully enjoy freedom in our Christian walk unless we are ready to forgive those who have hurt or offended us. This is an extremely important and serious issue, and one that we should not treat lightly, for when we fail to forgive those who have offended us, we break the bridge over which God's forgiveness flows into us.

FURTHER STUDY

Luke 17:1–10;
Mark 11:25;
Col. 3:13;
Eph. 4:32

1. What did Jesus teach on forgiveness?
2. What was the disciples' response?

Dear Lord Jesus, forgiving others is such an important and serious issue that I ask You to help see if I am harbouring any unforgiveness in my heart towards another and seek Your grace to forgive them. For Your own dear name's sake. Amen.

Getting to the root

FOR READING & MEDITATION – GENESIS 41:46–57
'God has made me forget all my trouble' (v51)

Yesterday we discussed the serious and important issue of extending the forgiveness we have received from God towards those who have hurt us or trespassed against us. Today, we get to the root of this.

Some say, 'I can forgive, but I can't forget'. But you don't really mean that, do you? See how this statement from the Lord's Prayer looks when set against that attitude: 'Father, forgive me as I forgive others. I forgive that person, but I won't forget what they did. You forgive me the same way. Forgive me, but don't forget my sins, and when I do something wrong, bring up the whole thing again.' God cannot, and does not, forgive that way. He blots the offence out of His book of remembrance. Perhaps you say: 'Well, I'll forgive, but I'll have nothing more to do with that person.' Now pray the Lord's Prayer with that in mind: 'Father, forgive me as I forgive others. I forgive that person, but from now on I'll have nothing more to do with them. You forgive me in the same way. Forgive me, but have nothing more to do with me.' Can you see the contradiction?

Don't try to forget things, don't try to smooth them over, and don't drive them into the subconscious. Get them up and out. A woman visited her doctor and asked him to give her a special ointment to smooth over her abscess. When the doctor refused and said it must be lanced, she left his surgery and went home. In a few days the poison had spread through her system and killed her. Unbelievable? The lady was known to me. I urge you, when facing the issue which is confronting you this week, don't ask for a sticking plaster or a halfway measure. Get it out. Forgive.

FURTHER STUDY

Gen. 45;
Phil. 3:13;
Heb. 8:12

1. How did Joseph demonstrate true forgiveness?

2. How did he see God's purposes in what had happened?

Heavenly Father, albeit gently and tenderly, help me to face this difficult reality. I would escape, but You won't let me. Today, therefore, in Your name, I want to forgive all who have hurt or injured me. It's done. In Jesus' name. Amen.

The journey to wholeness

FOR READING & MEDITATION – EPHESIANS 4:17–32

'Be kind... to one another, forgiving each other, just as in Christ God forgave you.' (v32)

If we are to grow spiritually and live in the fullness that God desires for us, we not only need to experience divine forgiveness for our own issues and sins, we do so as we extend forgiveness to those who have offended us.

Perhaps you might be saying at this moment: 'But I can't forgive: I have been hurt too deeply.' Then, may I say it very tenderly, but very solemnly, our creator and our all-knowing, all-wise, all-holy and all-loving heavenly Father knows best how the human personality was created to work – and when

FURTHER STUDY

Matt. 18:21–35;
5:7;
Luke 6:36;
Prov. 3:3

1. How does this parable apply to us?

2. What is the basis of forgiving others?

we hold unforgiveness in our hearts, we begin, slowly but surely (like grit in the cogs of a machine) to find it harder and harder to function. And one day, if the issue is not addressed, our personality will suffer a breakdown. If unforgiveness is something you are struggling with' today, then the place to start, as with any difficulty, is to be honest with God. You'll find your Father unsurprised and, as the prodigal son discovered, waiting with open arms to receive you. Ask God to fill your heart and mind with a fresh revelation and experience of just how much you have been forgiven.

We were designed to forgive from a place of forgiveness. This is an extremely difficult and delicate matter. To paraphrase C.S. Lewis, 'forgiveness is a wonderful thing until there's someone to forgive.' This may be the beginning of a journey for you today, and you may need others to walk with you. As we take these initial steps in forgiving those who trespass against us, God will take our hands and walk with us to lead us through to complete wholeness and restoration.

Lord Jesus, You who forgave those who spat in Your face and nailed You to a cross, help me to open my heart now, and forgive all those who have hurt me. I do it in Your strength and power. Thank You, Lord Jesus. Amen.

'If you have been particularly affected by this page, you may find it helpful to read Ron Kallmier and Sheila Jacobs, *Insight into Forgiveness* (Farnham: CWR, 2008).

A knotty problem

FOR READING & MEDITATION – JAMES 1:2–18

'God cannot be tempted by evil, nor does he tempt anyone.' (v13)

We move on now to examine the third petition in that part of the Lord's Prayer that focuses on ourselves: 'And lead us not into temptation, but deliver us from evil' (ESV). The first part of the Lord's Prayer relates, as we saw, to God and His glory. The second part relates to human needs. Here, in this third petition relating to our needs, the vital core of human need is touched, as Jesus once again shines a light on one of the deepest needs of the spirit – deliverance and protection.

An immediate problem, however, presents itself in these words, and it is one over which theologians have debated for centuries. The problem is this: if temptation is necessary to our growth (as we grapple – we grow), are we really expected to pray that God will not do what He must do in order to accomplish His work within us? After all, we are told, Jesus was led by the Spirit into the wilderness to be tempted by the devil.

Over the years I have had more letters about this particular issue than probably any other subject. One such letter put the problem like this: 'If, as I understand it, the word temptation (Greek: *peirasmos*) means a test or a trial, why should we pray to be kept from it, particularly as James tells us to "count it all joy when you fall into temptation"?' You see the difficulty I am sure. There are a number of interesting answers to this question, which we shall look at over the coming week. As this is one of the most confusing issues in Scripture, we need to approach it with a good deal of dependency on the Holy Spirit so that He might illuminate our minds and guide us into all truth.

FURTHER STUDY

Matt. 4:1–11;
2 Cor. 2:11;
Eph. 6:13;
1 Pet. 1:5–7;
2 Pet. 2:9

1. What is the basis of temptation?

2. How does this become sin?

Father, as I come up against this problem, which Your people have debated and discussed for centuries, help me, I pray, to come to clear and certain conclusions. In Jesus' name. Amen.

Unrecognised temptation

FOR READING & MEDITATION – MATTHEW 26:36–54

'Watch and pray so that you will not fall into temptation.' (v41)

We ended yesterday by saying that the words of Jesus in the Lord's Prayer – 'lead us not into temptation' – present a problem which has engaged the attention of theologians down the centuries. This week we shall examine some possible answers to the dilemma presented in these words, namely, why should we ask God to keep us from something that could work for our good?

One answer to this problem is that Jesus, when using these words, meant not just temptation but unrecognised temptation.

FURTHER STUDY

Gen. 3;
1 Thess. 3:5;
2 Cor. 11:3;
2 Pet. 3:17

1. Why did Eve succumb to temptation?

2. What is Paul's warning?

The advocates of this interpretation say that when temptation is recognised, it can be resisted, and when it is resisted, it then becomes a source of strength and resilience in our lives. One writer, who holds to this interpretation, put it this way: 'If I am filling out my income tax form, and I know that some income has come to me through other than the usual channels, and there is no way of anyone checking it, I am confronted with a temptation to omit it. But I know that is wrong. No one has to tell me. I know it. And when I resist the temptation, I find I am stronger the next time, when an even larger amount may be involved.'

There is a good deal of merit in this interpretation, for there is no doubt that temptation can be more effectively resisted when it is clearly recognised. Simon Peter is an example of this. Jesus said to him in the Garden of Gethsemane: 'Watch and pray so that you will not fall into temptation.' Sadly he did not heed that word and became involved in a serious act of violence (John 18:10). Peter thought he was doing the right thing, but really the violence was due to his inability to recognise what was happening.

Father, this may not be the exact meaning Your Son had in mind when He gave us these words, but I see that it has some application to life. Help me to be alert to every temptation and deal with it in Your strength and power. Amen.

FOR READING & MEDITATION – 1 CORINTHIANS 10:1–13

'God is faithful; he will not let you be tempted beyond what you can bear.' (v13)

We saw in our meditations yesterday that one interpretation of the words of Jesus in the Lord's Prayer – 'lead us not into temptation' – is that it refers to unrecognised temptation. If we pray for the ability to recognise temptation when it comes our way, then we will be able to confront it, and turn it to advantage.

Another interpretation of these words of Jesus is that this is a prayer for us to be kept back from more temptation than we can cope with. It's like saying, 'Lord, help us not to get involved in more temptation than we can handle.' This interpretation, as I am sure you can see at once, makes good sense, and could well be what Jesus meant.

One of the biographers of Hudson Taylor, the intrepid missionary to China, tells how, in his early days in that land, Hudson Taylor met with several great disappointments. One day, after a spate of troubles, he took hold of a guide who had demanded an outrageous fee from him and shook him violently. A few hours later, he realised he had responded badly, and after searching his heart for the reason why he had succumbed to anger and violence, he realised that he had been so preoccupied with his problems that he had failed to commit his ways to the Lord. His biographer says: 'If Hudson Taylor had prayed the prayer, "Lead us not into temptation", and committed his ways to the Lord, then perhaps the Spirit would have been able to direct his path so that he would not have faced more temptation than he could bear.' It is an intriguing thought. But is it the fullest meaning of Jesus' words? Possibly – but, as we shall see tomorrow, I think it means much more.

FURTHER STUDY

Acts 5:1–11;
Prov. 1:10; 4:14;
Rom. 6:13

1. Why did Ananias and Sapphira yield to temptation?

2. What is Paul's antidote?

Father, though the meaning of this phrase is not yet clear, one thing is – I need Your help at every stage of my earthly pilgrimage, for I cannot face temptation alone. So stay with me – every day and every hour. Amen.

God's safety valve

FOR READING & MEDITATION – HEBREWS 2:5–18

'Because he himself suffered when he was tempted, he is able to help those who are being tempted.' (v18)

Having looked at two different interpretations of the words 'lead us not into temptation' over the past few days, we come now to consider a third possible view, and one which I personally regard as the clearest meaning of Jesus' words. This interpretation was originally given by Chrysostom, an early Church father of the fourth and fifth centuries. He said: 'This particular petition is the most natural appeal of human weakness as it faces danger. It's the cry of a heart that despises and abhors even the possibility of sin. It is the admission of human weakness, and a recognition of our human tendency to stumble on into folly.'

FURTHER STUDY

Phil. 2:1–11;
Rom. 8:3;
Heb. 4:15;
2 Cor. 12:9

1. What is revealed through Christ's humanity?

2. How is this a strength to us?

Perhaps, in order to see these words of Chrysostom in a clear light, we need to set them against Jesus' experience in the Garden of Gethsemane. He prayed, 'Father, if it be possible, let this cup pass from me' (Matt. 26:39). Jesus knew that the only way to accomplish redemption for the human race was by way of the cross. Nevertheless, because He was human as well as divine, He gave expression to His humanity, even though, as the writer to the Hebrews said, He endured the cross for the joy that was set before Him (Heb. 12:2).

You see, even though Jesus knew that the cross had to be experienced in all its pain and torment, if men and women were to be redeemed, He still gave expression to His human feelings of dread and apprehension. Jesus did not feel guilty about this demonstration of His humanity, neither was God disappointed by His words, 'Father, if it be possible, let this cup pass from me.' If it was necessary for the Son of God to express His humanness in prayer, then it is a necessary part of our prayer too.

Father, I think I am beginning to see. These words are the safety valve, built into prayer, which enables me to express my weakness and my true feelings. I am so thankful. Amen.

God of the Unexpected

Though we can trust completely in our faithful and unchanging God, He is in no way limited by our expectations. Sometimes we can miss what God is doing because He is working in ways – or through things, people or situations – that we didn't at all expect.

This was particularly true of Jesus' coming to earth as a baby, when God chose to send the Saviour of mankind to be born into poverty instead of a palace. Next issue, we look at some of God's unexcepted interruptions in our lives. Join us to discover that when we trust in God whatever our circumstances, and allow Him to challenge our perceptions and change our thinking, life with Him can be an adventure.

Every Day **with Jesus**

NOV/DEC 2019

God of the Unexpected

'Call to me and I will answer you and tell you great and unsearchable things you do not know.'
Jeremiah 33:3

Living life with Jesus. Every day

CWR

Also available as an eBook/eSubscription

Obtain your copy from CWR, a Christian bookshop or your National Distributor.
If you would like to take out a subscription, see the order form at the back of these notes.

'Not cognitive, but emotional'

FOR READING & MEDITATION – HEBREWS 4:12–16

'For we do not have a high priest who is unable to sympathise with our weaknesses' (v15)

We continue exploring the words of Jesus in the Lord's Prayer, 'lead us not into temptation, but deliver us from evil'. Yesterday we touched on the fact that one explanation of these words might be that Jesus was providing a framework through which we could express our feelings of inadequacy and humanness when faced with the possibility of temptation.

One writer says of the words 'lead us not into temptation' that: 'They can only be properly understood when they are seen, not as cognitive (mental) but emotional.' He meant that this statement of Jesus is not intended to be something that appeals to the mind, but something that appeals to the heart. It is as if Jesus is saying: 'Even though your mind understands that as you face temptation and overcome it, you become stronger in God, there is still a part of you – your emotions – that feels it would rather not face the pressures. I understand this. I have been in that situation myself. So I will provide a prayer framework for you that will enable you to express, not so much your thoughts, but your feelings. It will be an admission of your fragility and mortality, it will also be a release, for if your fears are not expressed, they will be repressed, and will go "underground" to cause trouble. So these words will provide you with what you need – an opportunity to give vent to your inner feelings of reluctance at facing temptation.'

The more I ponder this, the more grateful I am to God for recognising that I am not just an intellectual being but an emotional being, and for building into His pattern of prayer a safety valve that lets me express my inner feelings.

FURTHER STUDY

1 Cor. 10:1–13;
Luke 22:31–32;
Rom. 16:20;
Heb. 7:25

1. What is the way of escape?

2. How can temptation be turned to good?

Father, what can I say? You think of everything. I am overwhelmed with the compassion that You show me, even when attempting to bring me to a higher level of prayer. Amen.

Acknowledge your feelings

FOR READING & MEDITATION – PSALM 42:1–11

'Why are you downcast, O my soul? Why so disturbed within me?'
(v5)

We saw yesterday that the statement, 'lead us not into temptation', is framed not to appeal so much to the mind, but to the emotions. Rationally, I may perceive that temptation does a perfecting work in my personality, yet in my feelings, if I am honest, I would prefer not to face it. Our emotions, as well as our intellect, are taken into consideration by Jesus when laying down for us this pattern of prayer, for He knows that to deny our feelings is to work against the personality and not with it.

It's widely accepted that the denial of feelings can contribute to the development of mental health problems. Negative feelings must be handled carefully for, if repressed, they are like the stories of pirates of past ages who would hide in the hold of a vessel and then rise up when the ship was out on the open sea in order to attempt to capture and possess it. Inevitably, a fight followed, as it will in the personality.

One of the most fascinating and helpful insights I have ever found in my study of human personality is the fact that we don't have to act on our negative feelings, but we do have to acknowledge them. If we say with our minds, 'Come on, temptation, I'm ready for you', and deny the fact that our emotions feel differently, then this pretence that the feelings are not there invites trouble into the personality. When, however, we acknowledge the feelings and admit they are there, we rob them of their power to hurt us. I see this psychological mechanism wonderfully catered for in the words of Jesus that we are considering. They are the framework in which our feelings can have a vote also. Thus, though not acted upon, they are not denied.

FURTHER STUDY

1 Kings 19;
Psa. 28:7;
40:17;
Isa. 41:10

1. How was Elijah able to express his feelings?

2. How did God respond?

Father, how can I thank You enough for taking into consideration every part of my personality in this exciting pattern of prayer. I am so thankful. Amen.

Evil is bad for us

FOR READING & MEDITATION – ROMANS 12:9–21

'Love must be sincere. Hate what is evil; cling to what is good.' (v9)

We shall spend one more day considering the words, 'lead us not into temptation, but deliver us from evil' (ESV). Today we concentrate on the last words of the statement – 'deliver us from evil'. Please notice it's not a prayer for deliverance from this or that type of evil, but evil itself. To Jesus, evil – whether in the evil of the flesh, evil of disposition, whether in the individual or the corporate will or, as the NIV translates this verse, from the 'evil one' himself – whatever form it takes, evil is never good.

FURTHER STUDY

Gen. 39;
1 Cor. 10:6;
1 Thess. 5:22;
1 Pet. 3:11;
2 Tim. 2:22

1. How did Joseph resist temptation?

2. What did Paul advise Timothy?

Eugene Patterson's translation of this verse in *The Message* is both illuminating and helpful: 'Keep us safe from ourselves and the Devil'. We certainly need saving from ourselves. So often we think we know best, reaching for self-dependence. For many of us, we find out how not to live the hard way. Thinking we know better than God, we set up and follow paths of our own choosing, only to find, like rats in scientific experiments, that some paths lead to dead ends and long-term personal difficulties and the occasional shock!

As we've already noted, many of society's problems are a product of our own making, as they are a result of greed or reaching for power. Many physical and health issues result from lifestyle choices. God has made it impossible for us to live against His design, or harm ourselves without His protest. He only protests because He loves us. Someone has pointed out that the word 'evil' is the word 'live' spelt backwards. Evil, then, could be said to be anti-life. The best way to deal with evil is to keep away from it, hence the prayer 'lead us not into temptation, but deliver us from evil.'

My good and gracious Father, You who made me for good, because goodness is good for me, help me to stay close to You, hate evil and avoid every kind of it. For Your own dear name's sake. Amen.

The doxology

FOR READING & MEDITATION – REVELATION 11:15–19

'The kingdom of the world has become the kingdom of our Lord and of his Christ, and he will reign for ever and ever.' (v15)

We come now to the final section of the Lord's Prayer: 'For yours is the kingdom and the power and the glory, for ever. Amen.'

This part of Jesus' pattern of prayer – a doxology – is so beautiful that it somehow seems almost irreverent to try to dissect it. Some believe that Jesus did not actually say these words. They claim that they were added by someone else at a later date, which is why they are not included in some versions of the Bible or it is put in a footnote. Some manuscripts have it, and some do not. I have looked long and hard at the evidence for and against their inclusion in the sacred Scriptures, and I am perfectly satisfied myself that they were part of Jesus' original pattern of prayer. There is almost an equivalent to these words in David's prayer in 1 Chronicles 29:11.

The prayer ends, as it begins, with an assertion of God's majesty and glory 'yours is the kingdom'. I believe that the emphasis here should be placed on the word 'is' – 'yours *is* the kingdom' – now. Despite all appearances to the contrary, God has never abdicated His position as ruler of the universe. What a heartening thought that is in these days, a thought to fill the soul with song, and flood the heart with hope and gladness. It is true that as a result of humankind's greed and lust for power there are many things in the world that militate against His authority, like war and poverty. These things may seem a flat and final refutation of the phrase 'yours is the kingdom', but their days are numbered. The hour will come when the kingdom of this world will signal its final surrender and have to bow before its rightful and sovereign Lord.

FURTHER STUDY

Matt. 4:1–11;
Obad. 21;
Heb. 12:28;
2 Pet. 1:11

1. Why was Satan's temptation foolish?

2. How did Jesus respond?

Father, help me to see, despite all the situations and circumstances which might resist Your eternal kingship, that You are reigning over the world now. Yours is the final control. I am so thankful. Amen.

'Their days are numbered'

FOR READING & MEDITATION – 2 THESSALONIANS 2:1–12

*'then the lawless one will be revealed, whom he Lord Jesus will…
destroy by the splendour of his coming.' (v8)*

We continue meditating on the final words of the Lord's Prayer. We said yesterday that, despite all evidences to the contrary, God is ultimately in charge of the world's affairs. He has set a rescue plan in action and manmade kingdoms on earth are numbered. Our God reigns! The 'power and the glory' spoken of in this doxology are kingdom power and glory. The other type of power and glory, that which is measured by earthly standards alone, and rejected by Jesus in His temptation in the wilderness, is destined to dissolution and decay.

FURTHER STUDY

Eph. 6:10–18;
John 12:30–31;
Heb. 2:14;
1 John 3:8

1. What is Paul's exhortation?

2. How can we take dominion?

Ezekiel the prophet, speaking centuries ago of the impermanence of anything not founded on kingdom values, said: 'The day is here! It has come! Doom has burst forth, the rod has budded and arrogance has blossomed' (Ezek. 7:10). Note the steps: doom bursts forth, sin has budded and arrogance has blossomed. And the fruit of all this? Dissolution and decay.

I am particularly fond of Moffatt's translation of 2 Thessalonians 2:3. When speaking of a prominent figure, who will arise in the last days and challenge the authority of God's kingdom, he refers to him as 'the Lawless One, the doomed One'. Those who are lawless, who resist and push against the laws of God's kingdom, which are written into the very nature of things, are doomed. Perhaps not today, nor tomorrow, but inevitably anything that is against God's kingdom is destined to destruction. It carries within itself the seeds of its own self-destruction and degeneration.

Our enemy's days are numbered – he will be overthrown by the splendour of Jesus. His is the kingdom, the power and the glory, for ever and ever.

Gracious Father, I am weary of looking upon the kingdom of the world. But when I lift up my eyes to look on You I see wholeness. Let me fix my gaze on You and see You, not as a reclining God, but as a reigning God. Hallelujah!

He reigns – NOW

FOR READING & MEDITATION – ROMANS 11:33–36

'To him be the glory for ever! Amen.' (v36)

We are seeing that the closing sentences of the Lord's Prayer, which (as we said) is really a doxology, contains a categorical assertion that God reigns through His kingdom – now. It manifestly requires a measure of faith and courage to affirm that truth in our modern society, when so many things seem positively to shout against it – so many wrongs that clamour for redress, so many problems that demand a solution and so many social issues whose existence appear utterly incompatible with the reign of God. Yet affirm it, we do.

A dear Christian lady in a letter to me some time ago said: 'I look around the world and am appalled. My only comfort is the hymn "Jesus shall reign where'er the sun." I, therefore, sit back and watch and wait the day.' I told her that her letter reminded me of a parody of an old hymn I heard someone put together in a conference once:

FURTHER STUDY

Rev. 7:9–17;
Exod. 24:17;
40:34;
Psa. 19:1;
John 1:14

1. How can we behold His glory?

2. How is our vision of God enlarged?

> *'Sit down, O men of God!*
> *His Kingdom He will bring,*
> *Whenever it shall please His will.*
> *You need not do a thing!'*

In my reply I said: 'Yes, it's true that one day the kingdom of God shall "stretch from shore to shore", but let us not ignore the fact that God is reigning now. Given our consent and co-operation, the kingdom of God can greatly affect the world through our committed lives. When we fail to see this, then it is possible that we struggle and stumble through life, waiting for Him, while all the time He is waiting for us.'

Lord God, deliver me from a view of life that says, 'Look what the world is coming to'. Help me to look at You, then I can say, 'Look what has come to the world'. Thank You, Father. Amen.

'Rise up, O men of God'

FOR READING & MEDITATION – PSALM 93:1–5

'The LORD reigns' (v1)

Quietly we are thinking our way through the truth that, although the fullness of God's kingdom is yet to come, there is a sense in which the King is reigning now, and we can say with the utmost certainty, 'The LORD reigns, he is robed in majesty; the LORD is robed in majesty and armed with strength' (v1).

Yesterday I mentioned about a lady who had written to me, indicating her intention to withdraw from life and await the day when God would finally establish His kingdom in power and glory on the earth. I replied with a parody of a hymn that apparently got her thinking. She wrote back a few weeks later and said: 'You were right. I was waiting for God, but now I realise He is waiting for me.' She ended her letter with the real words of the hymn:

'Rise up, O men of God!
Have done with lesser things;
Give heart and soul and mind and strength
To serve the King of kings.'

This, not the parody I referred to yesterday, indicates our line of action. Yes, of course, the final ushering in of God's kingdom is yet to take place, but that does not mean that He is taking a back seat in the world's affairs. God wants to reign through us! We need not wait for the day when dramatically and spectacularly the great God of the universe exercises His final authority. As through these closing pages of *Every Day with Jesus*, He sounds forth a rallying cry, respond to it, I urge you, with a fresh consecration of purpose, and dedicate yourself to letting Him reign through you.

FURTHER STUDY

Rom. 13:1–14;
2 Cor. 10:4;
1 Tim. 1:18;
6:12;
2 Tim. 2:4

1. How can we overcome the works of darkness?

2. What was Paul's exhortation to Timothy?

My God, I see everything clearly. I give myself wholly to You, not only just to live in me, but to reign through me. I gladly submit my whole being to You today. Live and reign in me. In Jesus' name. Amen.

'Follow the King'

FOR READING & MEDITATION – PSALM 96:1–13

'Say among the nations, "The LORD reigns."' (v10)

Over the past few days we have been saying that when Jesus uttered the words – 'For yours is the kingdom and the power and the glory, for ever, Amen' – it is to be seen as an assertion of God's kingly rule – now. The Almighty has never abdicated His throne. He rules – and our task, as His followers, is to affirm this in our attitudes, our behaviour and in our daily living.

On this penultimate day of a series in which we have been focusing on the Lord's Prayer, we ask ourselves: what practical steps can we take to substantiate our assertion that God reigns now? Out of many possibilities, let me just focus on two.

We can do it by our speech. Even though so many ugly and obtrusive facts seem to influence against the truth, we can explain to men and women that, behind the disordered events of this age, God is at work. We can do it also by our lives. The greatest contribution we can make individually to the world at this present time is to demonstrate, by our lives, that the King of heaven is reigning in us. High-principled, sacrificial and serviceable living is an irrefutable argument for the fact of God's loving rulership in the world. Tennyson put it in these words:

FURTHER STUDY

Rev. 19:1–10;
Exod. 15:18;
2 Chron. 20:6;
Psa. 24:10

1. What was the great multitude proclaiming?

2. What did it sound like?

> 'Follow the Christ – the King!
> Live pure! Speak true! Right wrong!
> Follow the King! Else wherefore born?'

The best guarantee we can give to a sceptical world that 'blessings abound where'er He reigns' is that those eminently desirable results have actually been at work in our own lives.

My Father and my God, I want to be at my very best for You. Help me depend on You. I offer my life again to You. May others see You ruling and reigning in me. For Jesus' sake. Amen.

We give – He gives

FOR READING & MEDITATION – EPHESIANS 4:17–32
'put on the new self, created to be like God' (v24)

We come now to our last day together, having examined phrase by phrase these amazing words of this pattern for prayer that the Lord taught His disciples.

Honesty compels me to admit that in studying the Lord's Prayer my personal approach to prayer underwent a complete overhaul and I brought my praying more in line with Jesus' pattern than ever before. After many decades as a Christian, I realised just what I had missed. Prayer to be effective flows out of a truly committed heart: it must be the definition of our spirit, our attitude to God.

FURTHER STUDY

Mark 6:45–56; 1:35; Luke 11:1; 5:16; 6:12

1. What was the pattern of Christ's life?

2. What was the disciples' request? Make it yours today.

An unknown author put it this way: 'I cannot say "our" if I live only for myself. I cannot say "Father" if I do not try to act like His child. I cannot say "who art in heaven" if I am laying up no treasure there. I cannot say "hallowed be your name" if I am not striving for holiness. I cannot say "your kingdom come" if I am not doing all in my power to hasten that event. I cannot say "give us today our daily bread" if I am dishonest, or seeking something for nothing. I cannot say "forgive us our trespasses" if I bear a grudge against another. I cannot say "lead us not into temptation" if I deliberately place myself in its path. I cannot say "deliver us from evil" if I do not put on the armour of God. I cannot say "yours is the kingdom and the power and the glory" if I do not give the King the loyalty due to Him from a faithful subject. And I cannot say "for ever" if the horizon of my life is bounded completely by time.' The whole thrust of the Lord's Prayer is that when we give God His rightful place, He gives us our rightful place. But not before.

Father, thank You for sharing with me the insights of this prayer over these past two months. May I bring my praying more in line with Your praying. For the honour and praise of Your Son and Your holy name. Amen!

Order form

4 Easy Ways To Order

1. Phone in your credit card order: **01252 784700** (Mon–Fri, 9.30am – 4.30pm)
2. Visit our online store at **cwr.org.uk/shop**
3. Send this form together with your payment to: **CWR, Waverley Abbey House, Waverley Lane, Farnham, Surrey GU9 8EP**
4. Visit a Christian bookshop

For a list of our National Distributors, who supply countries outside the UK, visit cwr.org.uk/distributors

Your Details (required for orders and donations)

Full Name:	CWR ID No. (if known):
Home Address:	
	Postcode:
Telephone No. (for queries):	Email:

Publications

TITLE	QTY	PRICE	TOTAL
		Total Publications	

UK P&P: up to £24.99 = **£2.99**; £25.00 and over = **FREE**

Elsewhere P&P: up to £10 = **£4.95**; £10.01 – £50 = **£6.95**; £50.01 – £99.99 = **£10**; £100 and over = **£30**

Total Publications and P&P (please allow 14 days for delivery)	**A**	

Subscriptions* (non direct debit)

	QTY	PRICE (including P&P)			TOTAL
		UK	Europe	Elsewhere	
Every Day with Jesus (1yr, 6 issues)		£16.95	£20.95	Please contact nearest National Distributor or CWR direct	
Large Print *Every Day with Jesus* (1yr, 6 issues)		£16.95	£20.95		
Inspiring Women Every Day (1yr, 6 issues)		£16.95	£20.95		
Life Every Day (Jeff Lucas) (1yr, 6 issues)		£16.95	£20.95		
Mettle: 15–18s (1yr, 3 issues)		£14.75	£17.60		
YP's: 11–14s (1yr, 6 issues)		£16.95	£20.95		
Topz: 7–11s (1yr, 6 issues)		£16.95	£20.95		
Total Subscriptions (subscription prices already include postage and packing)				**B**	

*Only use this section for subscriptions paid for by credit/debit card or cheque. For Direct Debit subscriptions see overleaf.

All CWR adult Bible reading notes are also available in **eBook** and **email subscription** format. Visit **cwr.org.uk** for further information.

Please circle which issue you would like your subscription to commence from:

JAN/FEB MAR/APR MAY/JUN JUL/AUG SEP/OCT NOV/DEC *Mettle* **JAN–APR MAY–AUG SEP–DEC**

💬 How would you like to hear from us?

We would love to keep you up to date on all aspects of the CWR ministry, including; new publications, events & courses as well as how you can support us.

If you **DO** want to hear from us on email, please tick here [ ]

If you **DO NOT** want us to contact you by post, please tick here [ ]

Continued overleaf >>

You can update your preferences at any time by contacting our customer services team on 01252 784 700. You can view our privacy policy online at cwr.org.uk

Payment Details

☐ I enclose a cheque/PO made payable to CWR for the amount of: £ _____

☐ Please charge my credit/debit card.

Cardholder's Name (in BLOCK CAPITALS) _____

Card No. ☐☐☐☐ ☐☐☐☐ ☐☐☐☐ ☐☐☐☐

Expires End ☐☐ ☐☐   Security Code ☐☐☐

Gift to CWR   ☐ Please send me an acknowledgement of my gift   **C** ☐

Gift Aid (your home address required, see overleaf)

giftaid it   I am a UK taxpayer and want CWR to reclaim the tax on all my donations for the four years prior to this year **and on** all donations I make from the date of this Gift Aid declaration until further notice.*

Taxpayer's Full Name (in BLOCK CAPITALS) _____

Signature _____   **Date** _____

*I am a UK taxpayer and understand that if I pay less Income Tax and/or Capital Gains Tax than the amount of Gift Aid claimed on all my donations in that tax year it is my responsibility to pay any difference.

GRAND TOTAL (Total of A, B & C) ☐

Subscriptions by Direct Debit (UK bank account holders only)

One-year subscriptions cost £16.95 (except *Mettle*: £14.75) and include UK delivery. Please tick relevant boxes and fill in the form below.

☐ *Every Day with Jesus* (1yr, 6 issues)
☐ Large Print *Every Day with Jesus* (1yr, 6 issues)
☐ *Inspiring Women Every Day* (1yr, 6 issues)
☐ *Life Every Day* (Jeff Lucas) (1yr, 6 issues)

☐ *Mettle*: 15–18s (1yr, 3 issues)
☐ *YP's*: 11–14s (1yr, 6 issues)
☐ *Topz*: 7–11s (1yr, 6 issues)

Issue to commence from
☐ Jan/Feb   ☐ Jul/Aug   *Mettle* ☐ Jan–Apr
☐ Mar/Apr   ☐ Sep/Oct   ☐ May–Aug
☐ May/Jun   ☐ Nov/Dec   ☐ Sep–Dec

CWR Instruction to your Bank or Building Society to pay by Direct Debit

DIRECT Debit

Please fill in the form and send to: CWR, Waverley Abbey House, Waverley Lane, Farnham, Surrey GU9 8EP **Name and full postal address of your Bank or Building Society**

To: The Manager   Bank/Building Society

Address _____

Postcode _____

Originator's Identification Number

| 4 | 2 | 0 | 4 | 8 | 7 |

Reference
| | | | | | | | | | | | | | | | | | |

Instruction to your Bank or Building Society
Please pay CWR Direct Debits from the account detailed in this Instructio subject to the safeguards assured by the Direct Debit Guarantee. I understand that this Instruction may remain with CWR and, if so, details will be passed electronically to my Bank/Building Society.

Name(s) of Account Holder(s)

Branch Sort Code
| | | | | | | | |

Signature(s) _____

Bank/Building Society Account Number
| | | | | | | | | |

Date _____

Banks and Building Societies may not accept Direct Debit Instructions for some types of account

Learn new skills and explore your faith with our residential courses

Introduction to Christian Care and Counselling

This five-day course, formerly the Introduction to Biblical Care and Counselling, is an excellent foundation for anyone who wants to learn more about themselves and how to help others effectively. Ideal for those involved in pastoral care or thinking about counselling training.
Next course: **Mon–Fri, 28 Oct – 1 Nov 2019**

Woman to Woman

Designed for women of all ages, this course will help to equip you with the skills and insight you need to minister in a variety of settings – whether in ministry or church leadership, in the workplace or in running groups or events.
Next course: **Mon–Fri, 14–18 October 2019**

Weekend Residentials

Why not consider taking some time out to invest in your relationship with God – whether through our Bible Discovery weekends, helping you grasp more of the wonder of God's story, or our Inspiring Women weekends, with fantastic teaching, worship and fellowship. Dates throughout the year.

Courses are held at Waverley Abbey House, Farnham, Surrey.
Dates correct at time of printing.

To find out more about all our courses and to book, visit
cwr.org.uk/courses or call **01252 784719**.

Teach Us to Pray

Given in both Matthew and Luke's Gospel, the Lord's Prayer provides us with a pattern for prayer that encompasses acknowledging the holiness and presence of God, seeking His will, accepting His provision, and asking for forgiveness and strength.

Whether it is a prayer you pray daily, or words you've not visited for a long time, join us this issue as we take a closer look at the Lord's Prayer phrase by phrase, and begin to understand it as the disciples did when they first asked Jesus: 'Lord, teach us to pray'.

Originally written by Selwyn Hughes
(1928–2006)
Founder of CWR, Selwyn was an internationally acclaimed speaker and a widely published author. This issue has been selected from over 40 years of his world-renowned writing ministry.

Updated by Mick Brooks
Chief Executive and Ministry Director of CWR, Mick has been the Consulting Editor for *Every Day with Jesus* for over ten years, seeing it continue to minister to over half a million readers.

www.cwr.org.uk
/edwjpage

Free group resource available at **cwr.org.uk/extra**

UK EDITION: £3.25

ISBN 978-1-78259-977-7

9 781782 599777

ALSO AVAILABLE AS
EMAIL SUBSCRIPTION/EBOOK/KINDLE

CWR Applying God's Word to everyday life and relationships